Black Catalogue is published by PDG Books Ltd
Registered company number 5334818
www.pdgbooks.com

ISBN 1-905519-02-8 / 978-1-905519-02-6

PDG Books and Black Catalogue logos by Susan Birks
Cover design - Claire Gambles
Cover photographs - Lee Smith
Additional artwork - Paul Smith

Every reasonable effort has been made to contact the copyright holders
of photographs reproduced/adapted from '100 Years of Sunderland'. If
the publishers are contacted, acknowledgement will be made in any future
editions.

Printed by The Charlesworth Group

DEDICATED TO
SUNDERLAND SUPPORTERS
PAST, PRESENT & FUTURE

Black Catalogue

Sunderland supporters
The fans' perspective

Edited by Ken Gambles

PDG Books 2005

Thanks

Specific thanks are due to: Sunderland AFC, especially Clare Blakeman and Rob Mason the programme editor; to the Sunderland Echo and Ian Laws for their assistance; Claire Gambles for her typing expertise and cover design; and to Russell Pearce for the photographic and technological know-how involved in reproducing the photographs.

I would like to thank all the contributors and those supportive of the enterprise in so many ways. Special thanks are due to Lee Smith for his marvellous contemporary photographs involving the Stadium and Sunderland AFC, and to Alan Brett and John Yearnshire. The publishers, PDG Books, have been patient and helpful in ensuring that this collection does justice to our life-long love affair with this great club. I hope it will serve as a tribute to all past generations of Sunderland supporters and hopefully inspire those to come.

Ha'way the Lads.

Editorial

As I am sure is the case with most of us, one of the greatest pleasures in life is 'talking SAFC' whether it be at a branch meeting, with friends or someone you've just happened to meet in the pub. Over the years I've enjoyed countless amusing or unlucky stories that people have experienced whilst supporting the Lads.

At a North Yorkshire branch meeting the idea of this collection was born, and then, supported by the publishers, 'Black Catalogue' took shape as a tribute to us, the supporters, the life-blood of the club. The arrangement of the pieces did not arise until the enjoyment of reading them had faded and then it was decided to place them in loose geographical sequence of where the memories took place. We start with the North-East, moving on to Yorkshire, then the North West and N. Ireland, followed by Wales and the South, finishing in London, with one final piece from abroad.

I hope you enjoy reading the collection and I hope it manages to capture some of that specialness of being a supporter of this fine club and bears witness to our love of Sunderland AFC.

The poem by Alan Craggs which closes the selection seems to me to be a most appropriate and moving evocation of the history and passion involved in our support. Here's to the future!

Keep the faith,

Ken Gambles
NYSSAN
(North Yorkshire Sunderland Supporters' Association)

(Lee Smith)

It is a great honour to be asked to provide the foreword to this collection of thoughts from Sunderland fans. When I first arrived at the club I was asked 'Why Sunderland?' and my reply was quite simple – this is a proper club with real fans. The passion of Sunderland fans both during my time at the club and for many years before me has been truly inspirational. Through times both good and bad our fans have remained loyal and true – we win together, we lose together, that's what makes the club so special. The fans are the heart and soul of Sunderland Football Club and myself and the team are delighted to have achieved success for them.

Mick McCarthy,

Manager, Sunderland A.F.C.

The One and Only, Slim Jim

Barry Robson, Harrogate

Jim Baxter's footballing skills have been called many things: quixotic, maverick, devastating, stunning, spellbinding, a left foot like a magic wand; one could go on. With Rangers between 1960-65 he won a hatful of trophies and his ten of 34 Scottish caps with The Lads, still makes him today, Sunderland's most capped 'north of the border' player. When at Sunderland he was part of the 1967 Scotland team who humiliated world champions England at Wembley, taunting the opposition with his 'keepie-uppie' routine and even sitting on the ball at one stage!

There was one other activity at which he became legendary though – boozing. He would try to drink anybody under the table, sometimes winning, sometimes meeting oblivion before reaching that dizzy height. It is with both of those talents, drinking and the Beautiful Game that this story deals.

Do you remember Wetherell's Night Club, that den of iniquity on Bishopwearmouth Green at the bottom of Chester Road? In its heyday in the late sixties it boasted acts of the calibre of Tom Jones, Englebert Humperdinck, Del Shannon, Diana Dors, Bobby Vee, Bob Monkhouse and a host of other showbiz talent. It was the town's premier night spot.

Of course, it later deteriorated to a miserable level of seedy decrepitude, where your feet would stick to the carpets as you made your way to the bar and the hordes of cockroaches had to be chased away from the beer pumps with Dettol aerosol before the terrified barmaids would pluck up the courage to pull pints. When it nearly burned down in the early seventies, it was discovered that the foundations were orange boxes!

Such is the stuff of nostalgia; places like 'Wethies' would never be allowed to exist in today's health and safety obsessed society. Maybe that's a good thing, but nobody really cared in those days, as long as you could go out, get blotto and try your luck with the 'bewer'. I was a rookie bouncer there in the early months of 1967 and enjoying every minute of it. The casino ensured that there were Sunderland's equivalent of the high rollers coming in: the top cabarets meant the top totty wanted to be seen in attendance and of course that also made it a magnet for the young, virile members of Sunderland AFC's first team. The place was packed practically every night and things were buzzing.

Friday 3rd March 1967 was no exception; I can't remember who the cabaret was but there were long queues waiting to get in most of the evening. Of course if you were a celeb you could gain entrance through the back door that opened into a little known lane round the side of the Polytechnic Library, which is where the intrepid trio of James Curran Baxter, Robert Kerr and Baxter's cousin, George Kinnell came in. Baxter was polite, friendly and personable; Kerr was all of 20 years, 5'5", nine stone wet through and resembled a skinny, undersized 16 year old; but looks can really deceive. Kinnell was lean and mean and never said a word.

I'm not sure what manager Ian McColl's views on players clubbing and drinking the night before a game were, especially when that game was against the Mags at Roker Park, but the language would have been choice, Scottish and blue. As the night wore on my duties took me all over the club and I didn't catch sight of them, but the three were no doubt safely ensconced in some little nook where prying eyes couldn't spy on their imbibing.

It's 2.30 in the morning of the 4th and the place has virtually cleared. I'm at the front door waiting for the dregs to go home when a taxi driver sidles up. "Taxi for three", he says. We wait a bit and then at the top of the first landing, carrying for all intents and purposes a stiff, are Kerr and Kinnell. They gently carry the comatose Baxter down the stairs, out into the taxi and off they go. To be fair, the two Ks looked and sounded fairly sober, but Slim Jim was well and truly gone.

Twelve hours later, from 3pm that afternoon, I was privileged to witness the destruction of Newcastle United aided and abetted by the revived corpse, his cousin and the little, scrawny Dumbarton lad, who also netted two sweet goals. It was nearly a one-man show, with Baxter mesmerising the Newcastle players, displaying some of the most skilful and silky ball-play Roker Park saw that day. The 3-0 final score did not do Sunderland justice, they should have doubled the tally. A team effort, of course, wins games, but some players are more equal than others and in that 90 minutes Baxter dazzled.

The man's recuperative powers must have been amazing. To transform from dead drunk to midfield general in less than half a day, leaves me in awe and wondering how his career might have been if he was a fitness buff and went light on the tipples. In all he played 98 games for Sunderland and scored 12 goals.

The rest is history. He transferred to Nottingham Forest in December 1967 for a very short spell and then went back to Rangers until his retirement at the (by today's standards) early age of 31. Baxter became a pub licensee, not a good move considering his drink problem and went into alcoholic decline. His physical problems worsened, he endured two liver transplants in 1994, finally and tragically dying of cancer in 2001.

When you mention the name Jim Baxter to any Scottish football fan of a certain age, a sense of wonderment descends on them, even Celtic supporters. They will remind you that Pele once said of him that he should have been a Brazilian, and every modern Scottish player or manager of stature pays homage to him. They have erected a statue of Baxter in his birthplace of Hill o' Beath, Fife, and Scots want to name the bridge at the

New Wembley after Baxter, the taunter of England who were, "Humbled by an impudent genius".

But as a Mackem I would like to leave the last word to Mick Connolly who wrote on the Baxter tribute web-site, "Roker Park packed to the rafters and Slim Jim swaggering around. Both a joy to behold."

Sat. March 4th 1967   Att. 50,442   Roker Park   Division 1
Sunderland 3 v 0 Newcastle United
(Kerr 2, Mulhall)
Montgomery, Irwin, Harvey, Todd, Kinnell, Baxter, Kerr,
O'Hare, Martin, Herd, Mulhall.

Herd in the Fulwell

Pete Barker, Billingham

George Herd was a member of the 1964 promotion team, a very skilful and tricky forward who was a fitness fanatic known for his athleticism.

There was a pre-season friendly at Roker Park and the half time "entertainment" was provided by a touring Russian acrobat and gymnastic team. The finale was an amazing display of co-ordinated gymnastics involving pikes, somersaults, half twists, the lot. When it was finished the Russians all turned to a very unimpressed Fulwell for applause only to be met with a few seconds of stony silence followed by a rousing chorus to the

"Ilkley Moor" tune of 'George Herd can do all that, George Herd can do all that, George Herd can do all that.'

Man and Boy

Brian Patilla, Bury

1960-61. I was 13. My first season. It was the first match of the season. After wanting to go for some years I was finally allowed to attend my first match. I took the bus on my own from Leam Lane Estate, Gateshead (where we had just moved to and which was held to be safer for travelling to Sunderland than where we lived before) and found my way to the ground. I just followed the crowd. What an experience. I ended up in the Roker End and Sunderland won 2-0 against the Boro on a glorious summer afternoon. This had to be heaven. However I got seriously lost on the way home as I didn't realise there were two totally separate bus routes (to final destination Newcastle). I arrived home three hours late and got into trouble. It didn't matter. I was hooked. WOW!

In the early sixties I went to a game with my younger cousin Richard. We hitchhiked from Gateshead to Blackpool. We had many adventures along the way but sadly had no chance of making kick off. We read in a newspaper how poorly we, and Sharkey in particular, had played in losing 3-0. We decided to head home but the only ride we could get was to Carlisle in a lorry. We arrived there well after eleven, hungry and deflated. We wandered around for a while and huddled against the cold in a shop doorway. A kind policeman happened by so we had to explain our predicament and provide proof of identity – my glasses prescription. We eventually got a diesel train to Newcastle then set out to walk home. A passing police patrol car called us over and wanted to know what was in the haversack – it was two scarves, a bell and a Klaxon horn. "Was it much of a game?" "Nah, got beat 3-0 and Sharkey had a stinker." "On yer way lads." BUT WE STILL HAD A GREAT DAY!

1966-67. I was 19. Richard and me went to Blackpool on a supporters coach with two older guys from Sunderland we had met at home matches. After the match the beer at the Manchester Arms was not good so Richard and me went on to Vodka and Lime, recommended by our pals. We'd never drunk it before, but it was very nice indeed. No problem – till we left the pub – next thing we remember we had missed the lights (one reason for coming) and were well on the way home. Can't even remember the score. BRILLIANT!

9 Mar 1991. I went from our home in Bury (with daughter Sue) to the home game against Sheffield United. I didn't tell the family still living back home in N. East, as we couldn't be bothered to visit, but enjoyed Seaburn once more before the game. Before kick off we organised an early birthday message for Sue. When it was read out at half-time Sue went scarlet, yet she knew it was coming! My brother-in-law Dave and his son Paul just happened to be at the match (we had never known them go before) so we got a few annoyed calls afterwards.....oh, and we lost 1-0.

Boxing Day 1992. My daughter Sue and me set off early from Bury to go to game at Tranmere and played tapes (north-east songs and others) all the way. We went through the 'automatic' lane at Kings tunnel but didn't have the right money so held people up. When we arrived at the ground we thought it was a bit more quiet than previous year with plenty of parking and as we got out of car a bloke says, "You do know its been postponed?" We were shattered but got back in the car and went home through the Queens tunnel. Our manager, Malcolm Crosby was sacked shortly afterwards because the pools panel gave a home win, so actually it was because by not playing we fell into the bottom three; and his contract said they could sack him if this happened, so they did. STILL A CANNY DAY OUT LIKE!

The Demon

Billy Vincent, Sunderland

"Shack! Shack! Shack! Shack!"

What was that I was hearing? We were enjoying a marvellous game of football in our usual position at the Fulwell End, down at the bottom corner near the Paddock.

"Shack! Shack! Shack! Shack!"

This time the chant was louder. A chant, that is what it was; a bloody chant. I had never heard this before in my life. I could imagine it going on in a church or a synagogue but never a football stadium, especially Roker Park. A chant!

"Shack! Shack! Shack! Shack!"

There it was again. I turned around and it appeared that the whole bank of thousands upon thousands of people were enthusiastically roaring their demand and flinging their fists at the sky in a way that seemed irresistible.

The stadium was already bubbling over with delight at the bewitching performance that had been presented by the great Shack. It was often said he always kept his best displays of wizardry for the Arsenal games, they having turned him down as a boy, but this was pure magic.

All the week we had looked forward to the game against Arsenal, darlings of the Football Association, blue-eyed boys of the media. I recall how they came prancing out to start the game, in their blue and white away strip, telling the world in the most belligerent fashion, they had come up from London Town to show the boys from the sticks what football was all about.

Football is only a game, I know that, but the hairs stood up on the back of my neck when I saw the cant and arrogance of this mighty Arsenal squad of athletes. Obviously, Sunderland were only there to make the numbers up and be thankful if they did not receive a scudding, while the supermen took two points back to the smoke.

"Shack! Shack! Shack! Shack!" The chanting grew louder and more persistent.

The game had kicked off and both teams were excelling themselves. It was a football feast. The ball came to Shack, who was in the inside left position, about twenty five yards from goal. Whenever Shack received a ball it was his; it did not go in the air, nor forward and neither to the left nor to the right; it went where he decreed it to go, or lay it dead at his feet. He had as near as damn it perfect ball control. He glided past the first of the supermen, leaving him in utter confusion. By now he had reached the corner of the penalty box and dribbled around the next obstacle as if he were a lump of wood. Along the eighteen yard line he advanced and the next Arsenal defender appeared to step to one side not wanting to hinder the progress of the Sunderland forward. Shack half turned, his right boot flashed and the ball thundered past Swindin's outstretched body and into the back of the net. At that time Swindin was being advocated as England's next goalkeeper. If he had a net in front of goal as well as the one behind, Swindin could never have saved that shot.

Shack was a wizard!

It was the goal of a life-time. A consummate example of what Association Football should be all about. Then what happened? The crowd went daft. Who were the masters now? It was Sunderland showing the Mighty Arsenal what football was all about and we were doing it in such scintillating style. One up! We were elated.

They say lightning never strikes twice in the same place. It did for Arsenal that day. On the same spot as before, Shack received the ball. Again he beat an opponent on the way to the corner of the penalty area. Again he immaculately demolished two competitors on his way along the eighteen yard line and once more he turned to show the world how to comprehensively beat a top class goal keeper.

Shack was a demon!

Two up against the glamour boys of English football! Could life for a Sunderland football supporter be better?

The stadium was in uproar. Could these goals have been rehearsed before the match had started? Had Shack bribed half the Arsenal team to get out of his way whenever he got the ball? He turned it on that day, did Shack. All of his tricks were on show; his scissors runs, his back-heels, his knee traps; at one point in the game he stopped the ball and sat on it while he figured out his next move.

It all reached an apotheosis when the referee awarded Sunderland a penalty kick. We were in ecstasy. The chanting started and gradually swelled in crescendo. Arsenal had come to Wearside with more edge than a broken bottle and now we were taking the elite apart. When I say 'we', I mean the forty odd thousand of us in the stands, ten outstanding footballers dressed in red and white stripes or a green jersey and the devil himself who came to our ground every other week under the name of Shack.

"Shack! Shack! Shack! Shack!"

The crowd roared and the cries rolled down the Fulwell End and over the pitch.

"Shack! Shack! Shack! Shack!"

The demand was overpowering. Shack had to take the penalty. Shack had to have his hat-trick. We all know what Robbie Burns said about the best laid plans of mice and men and now we were about to see the same thing happen to our hastily and passionately arrived at decision. It had been decided somewhere else at another time that all our penalties were to be taken by Stan Anderson. No one was against Stan. He was one of our lads who we had brought up and would become a great footballer. It was terrible to see one so young walk over and take the ball and such a gigantic responsibility.

He missed.

As I walked out of the gates to start my long walk home, I rejoiced. We had beaten the unbeatable, we had two points in the bag, we had been gorged at a banquet of magnificent football. Yet, somehow, I failed to get that feeling of complete fulfilment because Shack didn't get the hat-trick he deserved.

Out of the mouths of babes...

Bill Allen

People often ask the question, 'What's your earliest recollection of life on earth?' This is mine. I am now 68 years of age having been born on 1st August 1937 and as we all know Sunderland won the FA Cup in that year. I was born in Frosterley, County Durham to where my parents had moved during the depression of the 1930s. My father was a fanatical Sunderland supporter.

I remember sitting on my mother's knee as she was trying to teach me the Lord's Prayer. I must have been about three or four years old. My father entered the room as my mother was repeating "Our Father which art in heaven etc." My Dad butted in and said, "Never mind teaching him that, teach him 'Mapson, Gorman, and Hall, Thomson, Johnston, McNab, Duns, Carter, Gurney, Gallacher and Burbanks'."

I must have been the only toddler alive who could recite the 1937 cup winning team BEFORE the Lord's Prayer!

Just the ticket

Peter Ede, Sunderland
(Name sounds familiar? Ed)

Frank, George, Bob and I had been friends since schooldays and we went everywhere together. Well, everywhere except football matches because George didn't like football. When it came to getting tickets for the Cup Final, only those supporters who were lucky enough to get the right voucher would be able to get a ticket. I remember when the four of us met up one day and Frank, Bob and I were ecstatic because we all had the right voucher. Frank even had two, so he could get two tickets. When he told us he had two, I remember George being excited that he could also go to the Final. There was a brief pause as Bob and I looked at each other. We knew what was coming even before Frank spoke. He looked at George and very calmly said: "Sorry bonny lad but my spare ticket has to go to a true supporter." I think George must have expected that because he didn't argue about it. He seemed to know that was the right thing to do.

Once we'd got the tickets, Frank put a notice up in Sunderland Poly, where he was a part-time student. He asked for a genuine supporter who didn't have a ticket to contact him. He got a few replies and he interviewed them to determine who was the most deserving of this, the greatest of all prizes for a Sunderland supporter. He then sold the ticket to the lucky applicant for the original purchase cost. He knew if he had made a profit on it he would be committing a mortal sin.

The night before the final we got the bus from Houghton to Sunderland. The coach to London was leaving at midnight but we arrived early so we could go to the pictures to see "A Clockwork Orange". When the film was over we made our way to Park Lane and were amazed to see at least half of the Fulwell End there. Having just watched one of the most horrifying street gang films of all time, we were a little apprehensive but we needn't have worried - it was party time! When our coach eventually started to slowly pull out of the station, Bob suddenly pointed out of the window shouting: "Look! Look!"

When we looked out we saw a skinhead with Doc Marten boots, tattoos, the whole lot. And he was crying his eyes out. Bob shouted out of the window to ask what was going on. "Couldn't get a ticket mate," he said, adding, "you'd better bring that cup back!"

"We will mate, we will."

And we did.

Sunderland-related comments from *The Book of Football Quotations* by Phil Shaw.

"He was so keen to join us at the hotel that he almost got there early enough to meet the last squad going home"

    Keegan (England manager) on Kevin Phillips

"I'm just as good as Schmeichel but I'm more modest by nature"

    Tommy Sorensen

"In football we all know that you stand still if you go backwards"

    Peter Reid

"Jim Baxter drove Alan Ball mad calling him Jimmy Clitheroe (a small, high-voiced comedian) but Bally couldn't get near enough to do anything about it"

    Billy Bremner on Jim Baxter v England in 1967

"Anyone who uses the word 'quintessentially' during a half-time team talk is talking crap"

    Mick McCarthy on Quinn's contribution to a 1998 international game.

"We call him Germ. He always has a cold or something"

    Darren Huckerby on Michael Bridges

One of the greatest away games I have been to has to be our famous victory over the Mags at St James' Park in 1979 when Gary Rowell wrote his name into SAFC folklore by scoring a magnificently executed hat-trick!

I've been to some cracking away games over the years in my time, but not many could beat the unbelievable experiences of that winter's afternoon in February, 1979 when Rowell ran riot on Tyneside. It was the days of long hair, flared trousers, punk music and Doc Marten bovver boots. Five of us met up early on that cold Saturday morning in our favourite watering hole, The Borough in Vine Place. The place was buzzing as loads of red and whites gathered for the biggest fixture in the calendar that season. After supping copious amounts of Vaux's famous brew, Double Maxim, it was off to Tyneside in my mate Geoff's sturdy old banger, although most fans had gone on a special train put on by British Rail.

On arriving on Tyneside we parked the car quite a distance from the ground. Being on our own and having to run the gauntlet of groups of Mags on every street corner, we hid our scarves under our denim jackets as we didn't want to die before we got old. Fuelled with the Dutch courage that is Double Maxim I recall cheekily saying to a few black and whites, "Alreet mate?" some replied, others just glared suspiciously. We heard fighting was taking place all over Newcastle as the Sunderland fans were starting to arrive on the football special trains from Wearside. The next day the media carried headline stories of clashes in the Pink Lane area near the railway station, at the Waterloo pub on Westgate Road, and on the petrol station forecourt behind the Gallowgate end. This was the days before video surveillance and better security. You literally took your life in your own hands, and the adrenaline was flowing constantly when you were in the enemy's territory; at any time you could be jumped by the Mags. It was like a mission, you had to get to the ground before they got you! The Mags were hunting in packs, and you had to keep your nerve, for, if you showed any fear they would be down on you like a pack of wolves!

As I was walking towards the ground, I visualised my scarf falling down from under my jacket. Good job I used to be a scout, and could tie good knots! But once inside the ground you felt at home with the rest of the travelling troops. The atmosphere was rocking, with about 8,000 red and whites in a crowd of about 35,000. We were packed in like sardines, as there was building work going on at the time, but the Fulwell End on tour blasted out all the top anthems, including the usual array of songs about not being mastered by the black and white bar stewards! It was like a scene from the famous film 'Zulu' with war cries going up constantly, and taunting the enemy in their own backyard. The crowd swayed back and forwards down the steep terracing and to be amongst it all was just great for a young whipper-snapper like me.

As Sunderland ran out in their sexy blue Umbro away kit, the scenes on our end were just mental. We gave them one hell of reception, and the lads were up for it, they knew they couldn't let us down, we had done our bit, now it was time to do theirs.

After only six minutes Gary Rowell had put Sunderland 1-0 up, after a Jeff Clarke free-kick was headed on by Chisholm and Rostron into his path, and he slipped it past Steve Hardwick. Cue madness and bedlam from the away fans with the Mags looking on in helpless anger and disbelief. Elliott and Clarke were in brilliant form in the middle of the back four against the Mags' number nine and supposed match-winner Peter Withe, and we were looking classy and in total control. The brilliant Kevin Arnott was creating magic all over the midfield, until suddenly he released Rowell with a defence-splitting wonderful pass and Rowell slotted it away past the helpless Hardwick with ease. TWO NIL to the lads! This was pure heaven! "Jingle Bells, Jingle Bells, Jingle all the way, oh what fun it is to see Sunderland win away" was the battle cry. My ribs were nearly broken after a massive Sunderland fan the size of the popular wrestler of the day, Giant Haystacks hugged me like some demented crazy man after our second goal had gone in. But so what? We were beating the Mags in their own back yard, and not many things in life gave you this type of buzz.

It was ten New Year's Eves all rolled into one! It was party time, and we were going to milk it big this time! My cup of steaming Bovril disappeared down some poor gadgie's neck at the same time as our goal, and his screams could be heard way back in Sunderland I think, he probably had third degree burns, the poor lad!

The match just got better and better from our point of view and the stunned Mags were about as loud as a group of nuns playing scrabble. We got the jitters when John Connolly pulled a goal back but referee Pat Partridge was ignoring some waist high tackles on Rowell and Entwistle, as the Mags were beginning to lose it. Then the tricky full back Micky Henderson was flattened in the box by a vicious tackle. Rowell stepped up to notch his hat-trick by slotting a cool penalty past the clueless Hardwick, 3-1. I was now standing on top of a crush barrier (like some nutter!) with my mates holding my ankles. The adrenaline was flowing, the disillusioned Mags were filing out in droves in embarrassment. The Fulwell End on tour was in full voice now, "We all agree Gary Rowell is magic!" rang out followed by a chant of "EASY! EASY! EASY!" I was conducting the Fulwell End choir (from my barrier vantage point) as though it was Last Night of the Proms. We were hungry and the natives wanted more. They duly obliged and when Entwistle banged in the fourth I fell off my podium and landed onto a group of lads, who cushioned my fall. It was party time again.

A gritty yet skilful performance had given everyone who witnessed it a truly memorable day out. We had a few dodgy moments going back to our car in the middle of Newcastle, as it was virtually impossible to look sad in amongst all of the gloomy Mags, who were queuing to hoy themselves off the Tyne Bridge, when the whole of your body was bursting with pride and happiness. They were on every street corner baying for the blood of any Sunderland fan. Fortunately we got back to the car unscathed, but driving back to Sunderland through Gateshead was good fun, I couldn't resist shouting out of the car window, "Did you enjoy your stuffing you turkeys!" The beer flowed in Sunderland all night, as we toasted King Rowell in style.

Sat 24th Feb. 1979   Att. 34,733   St James' Park   Division 2
Newcastle United 1 v 4 Sunderland
(Rowell 3 [1 pen], Entwistle)
Siddall, Henderson, Bolton, Arnott, Clarke, Elliott, Chisholm, Rostron, Entwistle, Lee, Rowell. Sub: Docherty.

Limp Response
Carol Little and Anne Birkbeck (sisters), Sunderland

My sister and I attend most home games and one of the highlights is going to the Stadium of Light early so we can ask the players for autographs, pose for photographs and ask if they are playing today. On one occasion we noticed Tore Andre Flo was walking with a limp. So my sister asked him, "Are you injured Tore? You seem to be walking with a limp"

To which he replied, "No.... I always walk like this!!!"

Could this be the reason why he became known as Tore Andre Flop?

Raich Carter – A Schoolboy Memory   Jerome Hanratty

In the late 30s Sunderland's successes sent their reputation ringing round the playground; and associated with the sound of Sunderland was that of a player: Carter. The two were as one to our ears.

My first sight of the pair of them came a few years later in November 1942; a game against Gateshead at Redheugh Park in the 'League North' (a wartime replacement for the Football League.) Carter, the captain was conspicuous not only for his outstanding ability and powerful left foot shooting (he seemed to take all the throw-ins, free kicks, and I think scored the only goal) but for the colour of his stockings. Sunderland at that time wore black and red stockings – but with wartime shortages the red had faded to a pale pink. Carter's, however, remained crimson.

A week or so later came my first 'big' game: the R.A.F against Scotland at St James' Park before a 40,000 crowd, not including a large number perched on the roof of the Leazes stand. Scotland had a strong looking team – largely filled with pre-war internationals – but the R.A.F won 4-0. Carter, with Stanley Matthews his partner on the right wing, scored the first three of them, a genuine hat-trick of bulleted shots. The other inside forward was Peter Doherty of Huddersfield Town, with the prolific Ted Drake in between them. Already an England international, Carter went on to win several war-time caps after this, before being posted abroad.

News of his arrival home on leave always boosted the gate at Roker, but in his absence there had been a transformation: the stockings remained red but the hair had gone snowy white. And if a transfer to Derby County at the end of the war might have seemed to some a pensioning off, it was a misconception he soon put right by winning a second Cup Winners' medal in the 1946 Final against Charlton alongside former partner Peter Doherty.

When League Football resumed on August 31st 1946, those same cup winners were coincidentally the visitors to Roker Park for the opening game. In the words of the match programme '…unless it had been our neighbours from Newcastle, it is doubtful whether we could have had more popular opposition.' Sunderland won 3-2 but Carter's revenge came a year later when he orchestrated a 5-1 defeat for Sunderland on the occasion of Len Shackleton's debut. Talk about motivation!

Since then there have been a few false starts and many lost hopes in Sunderland's search for a replacement. Can we envisage, in this present day a Sunderland born player – an inside forward (sorry, a midfielder) with a strong left foot – coming along to step into those shoes? A pair of socks is waiting.

Sat. August 31st 1946   Att. 48,666   Roker Park   Division 1
Sunderland 3 v 2 Derby County
(Burbanks, Whitehouse 2)
Mapson, Stelling, Jones, Willingham, Hall, Housam, Lloyd, Watson, Duns, Whiteburn, Burbanks.

Charlie's Angles

Charlie Hurley (Voted Player of the Century in 1979), Sunderland

My worst memory of playing for Sunderland came immediately after my transfer from Millwall. I was bought to shore up the defence, but we lost our first two games 7-0 at Blackpool then 6-0 at Burnley. Charlie Summerville, a reporter for the Mail asked me for my views about the problems after these two heavy defeats, so I said, "What do you mean?

You've seen an improvement already!" and he never forgot that answer. Unfortunately we were relegated that year, for the first time in the club's history.

Alan Brown gradually changed the team bringing in younger players such as Ashurst, Irwin, McNab, Hooper, Herd and Mulhall until eventually we won promotion back to the top division in 1964. An astonishing seven players in that team came through the youth system, a big change from today. I nick-named Alan Brown 'the Bomber' as he was very tough, and frightened the players with his sergeant-major-like approach, but we all knew what we had to do in the team. In the quarter-final of the FA Cup in 1964 we were drawn away at Manchester United and in the team talk before the game I asked Alan Brown who was going to stop Bobby Charlton, Denis Law and David Herd. He thought for a moment, looked at me and said, "I don't think you can do it on your own Charlie," which proved he had a sense of humour despite being a disciplinarian.

I always remember a bonus system he introduced. We would be paid £300 if we were in the top 2 after 10 games, the same after 20 and then again after 30 games. However, if we missed out after 10 games we could get it back if we were 2nd after 20 or 30. We were 3rd after 10 games, and 3rd after 20 so no money, but when we played Norwich at home in the 29th game a win would assure each member of the team £900 as we would be second. We beat Norwich 7-0 with Nick Sharkey scoring five, although eventually we missed out on promotion. The bonus system was quickly overhauled by Alan Brown – no more 10-20-30 – it was all or nothing at the season's end. The next season we were promoted!

This was undoubtedly the greatest day of my football career when we beat Charlton 2-1 at Roker Park and did a lap of honour in front of the fans. We went back to the dressing room, but a chant went up of 'Char-lie, Charlie' so we all went out again shaking hands with the miners and shipbuilders who formed the core of our support. It was an honour for the players – I will never forget it or the team I played with.

Sat. April 18th 1964   Att. 50,827   Roker Park   Division 1
Sunderland 2 v 1 Charlton Athletic
(Herd, Crossan)
Montgomery, Irwin, Ashurst, Harvey, Hurley, McNab, Herd, Crossan, Usher, Sharkey, Mulhall.

Dreamland

Steve Hart, Starbeck

1999-2000 this most extraordinary of seasons grew more extraordinary still by the week. Can you imagine how we all felt at half time in this game? Four-nil up against Chelsea after having watched some of the best football I have seen Sunderland play.

I expected Sunderland to be at Chelsea from the start, tackling, battling, not letting Chelsea establish any pattern, but what I didn't expect from the whistle was for Eric Roy to dance through a wave of blue shirts and cross for big Niall to put Sunderland ahead.

Chelsea did have the odd half chance. Flo - remember him? - swayed past Craddock but shot into the side netting; Zola manoeuvred some space but shot at Sorensen, yet Wise & co were being swamped in midfield by Thirwell's energy, Schwarz's reading of the game and Roy's competitiveness and astute passing.

Sunderland scored an outrageous second. The ball broke thirty yards out. One swing of Phillips' boot and the ball was soaring, swerving past de

Goey. No one scored a better goal anywhere that season.

Desailly, a World Cup winner with France last year, couldn't handle Quinn at all. Quinn outmanoeuvred him then chipped, de Goey produced a flying save, but Phillips was there to snaffle the rebound.

It became mayhem. Schwarz's cross led to Phillips' cross hitting his own player, Thirwell, to prevent a goal : then came Summerbee's corner and Quinn's volley at the far post, back across de Goey for number four. Pure unadulterated magic.

Down on the concourse at half time was a sea of stunned, happy faces after witnessing this breathless display of commitment, skill and passion. I first watched Sunderland in 1972 and this was definitely the best I had ever seen them play. Never had I had a better time at a football match and judging by the responses in the press and fanzines in the months that followed, nor had most of the people present on that most memorable of days.

Heart-stopping excitement

Les Watson, Jarrow

10.00 – It's the game we've all waited for. Sunderland are doing well and we're hoping to scrape a win against Chelsea who humiliated us 4-0 on the first day of the season. I've just come out of the shower. I'm sitting on the edge of the bed and have a pain in my chest – breathing is becoming difficult. I'm 51 years of age and it looks like the dreaded heart attack is happening. Why today?

10.20 – Breathing is very painful but my heart is still going, so maybe its not a heart attack after all. Should be fine by three o clock!

"Football or not, we are going to the hospital" insists my wife and I have reluctantly to agree. Thirty painful minutes later she has dressed me and I'm on my way down stairs. "Put my season ticket into my jacket and put it and my hat into the boot of the car," I plead. "It might be nothing and I'll be fine in an hour or so." I'm refusing to leave the house without the season ticket and my wife agrees to take it, although I know she is only humouring me and thinks that there's no chance I'll make it.

11.00 – A&E – surely the NHS can turn me around in four hours! I've seen the triage nurse and she has given me a high priority – more to do with the fact that they don't want a possible cardiac arrest on their hands rather than any sympathy for my tale of hoping to be at the match.

Midday –A boost – a porter comes and takes me along for an x-ray.

13.00 – Time is ebbing away, but suddenly a doctor appears with a file and some x-rays under his arm. He demonstrates his best bedside manner before launching into the evidence from the x-rays. "I'm sorry to inform you, but there is some serious damage to your lungs." The heart may be OK, but this is not the news I was expecting and exchange a nervous glace with my wife. "How many cigarettes do you smoke a day?" asks the doctor. "None, I reply I've never smoked in my life". "That's unusual", he replies, "these symptoms are typical of someone who has been smoking heavily for many years. Let me look in the file………..oh, very sorry I'm in the wrong cubicle." He leaves and we don't know whether to be relieved or angry. Anyway I'm in too much discomfort to be bothered.

14.00 –The correct doctor arrives this time and eventually diagnoses a muscle trapped between my ribs – must have done this by twisting my torso or something. It's easily remedied and will be eased immediately by means of an injection – but there is an emergency coming in and it may take some time to arrange. Some people are just too selfish; what can be more urgent than being on time to hear the Dance of the Knights?

14.50 –That's it, the injection is done and I'm preparing to leave. My wife has conceded that I am not dying and although bloody stupid to even think about it, able to go to the match if I insist. We're in the car. Its taken an age to get the jacket on in the car park and I'm keeping quiet about the pain in the chest.

15.35 –We arrive outside the SoL. My wife parks the car near the north stand where I can get in quickly and head for my seat in the West Stand. She puts my hat on me and pushes me in the direction of the gate.

15.40 –I'm through the gate and I can hear some noise – something has happened. I pass a steward at the bottom of the ramp and I ask him what is going on. He replies, "Not much, don't worry you haven't missed much." I get to the top of the ramp and look up at the scoreboard at the far end of the ground.

SUNDERLAND 4 CHELSEA 0

I look again. The injection must have blurred my vision! No, it's correct and my heart sinks. I turn to find the steward with the wicked sense of humour but he has gone. I hurry, with some discomfort, to my seat in Row 34 and my friends greet me with, "You have just missed the most brilliant 40 minutes of football we have ever seen at the SoL. Where have you been?"

"Well, you'll never believe it but…………….."

Sat. 4th Dec 1999   Att. 41,199   Stadium of Light   Premiership
Sunderland 4 v 1 Chelsea
(Phillips 2, Quinn 2)
Sorensen, Makin, Craddock, Williams, Gray, Thirlwell, Roy, Schwarz
Summerbee, Quinn, Phillips. Sub used: Holloway.

We are Sunderland

Time-honoured tradition of making your way to the match

Great Scots!

Slim Jim in action for Scotland v Brazil with No. 10 Pele (below)

SAFC 98 apps 12 g

Scots caps 34

George Herd in less acrobatic mode

SAFC 315 apps 55 g

Scots caps 5

Goal!

[A King/G Biggs]

Yeess! Celebrations following a Marco goal at Roker in 1990

Footy in the 60s

A very different looking Football Echo and plainer programme. The Charles Buchan football monthly no longer exists and was far less innovative than today's 'Four-Four-Two'. The Football League Review was given out free with match programmes at every ground and the cover here depicts centre half George Kinnell, Slim Jim Baxter's cousin and drinking partner.

SAFCSA began in 1965 and here are membership forms and associated booklets. The Black Cat ashtray has survived intact since about 1968. Subbuteo has been supplanted by playstation, and will we ever see another World Cup Winners stamp?

(R.Pearce)

The perfect atmosphere. The SoL at night.

(Lee Smith)

Shack and Jack

(Legend Len Shackleton, 'Shack' (left), a demon on his day and Jack Stelling (right) full-back in the Fifties who was surprised by a Mackem voice in Cardiff.)

Shack 348 apps (100 goals)   Jack 272 apps (8 goals)

Len Shackleton – a veritable genius whose ability to control and deliver a football has seldom been surpassed. He was very much a 'maverick' and not popular with the establishment hence a paltry 5 England caps. Dubbed 'The Clown Prince of Soccer', he famously left a blank page in his autobiography as testimony to the knowledge of football chairmen. Played his last game for Sunderland early in the season of our first ever relegation from the top flight.

Jack Stelling – an unsung hero of the post-war era. A right back noted for his bravery and consistent performances. Signed from Usworth Colliery during the war but played with many high-profile, expensive signings during our 'Bank of England' era. Sadly missed a twice-taken penalty against Man City – victory here in 1950 would almost certainly have guaranteed the League Championship. Almost a hero.

A Night with Niall

(R.Pearce)

Memorabilia from the marvellous 'Night with Niall', Darren Williams's shirt and Matt Holland's stocking tabs. A wonderful £1 million was raised for children's hospitals in Sunderland and Dublin thanks to Niall's generosity.

Niall Quinn, "The happiest days of my sporting life were spent at Sunderland. I learned my trade at Arsenal, became a footballer at Manchester City, but Sunderland got under my skin. It hurt me deeply to leave. I love Sunderland."
The Guardian 26th Aug 2005.

We'll keep the red flag flying high.

(Lee Smith)

King Gary. Gary Rowell for Sunderland v Man United in 1977 before his famous Mag-slaying hat-trick in 1979. Now commentates for Metro Radio with Simon Crabtree. A very popular (and no wonder) ex-player who regularly watched SAFC even before his media work.

(Courtesy SAFC)

Newcastle 1 Sunderland 9

YES, THE SCORELINE is correct. Believe it or not, England's top team — twice League champions and three times Cup-finalists in the last four years, and now challenging for the League title once more — have been beaten 9–1 at home by their neighbours.

There was no inkling that such a shock was in store at half-time, with the score at 1–1. But in the space of 28 second-half minutes, Sunderland hammered eight goals past the hapless Magpies, the last five coming in eight minutes. Newcastle were just stunned by the onslaught.

Sunderland have an excellent

George Holley, who scored a hat-trick for Sunderland.

recent record at St James's Park, having won seven of their last 10 League games there. But nothing could have prepared even their wildest fans for the goal glut to come after the interval. Newcastle-born Billy Hogg added another three to his first-half goal, and George Holley also helped himself to three.

With Everton beating champions Manchester United to go further ahead in the table, it remains to be seen whether Newcastle can recover from this extraordinary setback and keep up their challenge for the League title.

Sunderland's Cup at last

SUNDERLAND HAVE WON the FA Cup for the first time in their long and illustrious history. At long last, after a difficult campaign, they reached the final, and now, coming back typically from a half-time deficit, they have beaten Preston 3–1 at Wembley.

They needed a replay to beat Luton in the fourth round and two before they slammed Wolves

4–0 in the sixth. And they were a goal down against Third Division Millwall in the semi-finals before emerging 2–1 winners.

In what was by no means a great final, Preston's Scottish international centre-forward Frank O'Donnell put them ahead after 38 minutes. Sunderland, under the astute generalship of their captain and inside-right

Raich Carter, took charge in the second half, and Bobby Gurney equalized after seven minutes with a header following a corner. Carter put them ahead 20 minutes later from a Gurney pass, and shortly afterwards, Eddie Burbanks shot home from a narrow angle to clinch the match and the Cup for this talented, and delighted, Roker side.

Carter (striped shirt, behind goalkeeper Burns) puts Sunderland in front.

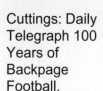

Cuttings: Daily Telegraph 100 Years of Backpage Football.

The Good Old Days

Sunderland attack (above) and defend (below) at the Stadium of Light.

(Photos: Lee Smith)

(A.King/G.Biggs)

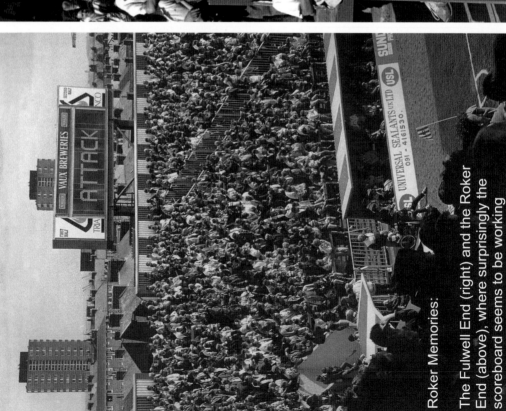

Roker Memories:

The Fulwell End (right) and the Roker End (above), where surprisingly the scoreboard seems to be working

Sunderland AFC 1965/6.

The free gift from Typhoo meant drinking a lot of tea to collect the tokens.

Neil Martin (left) has been added to the photo as he was signed from Hibs in October 65 for £45,000. He scored 46 goals in 99 games.

WITH THE COMPLIMENTS OF **Ty.Phoo** TEA LTD., BIRMINGHAM 5

SUNDERLAND F.C.

Back row, L to R: McNab, Parke, Harvey, McLaughlan, Hurley, Ashurst, Irwin

Front row, L to R: Hellawell, Herd, Hood, Sharkey, Mulhall

The First Cup Win

First-class passenger . . . Raich Carter arrives home with the FA Cup after Sunderland's 3–1 victory over Preston

Our first Cup success in 1937. Hendon-born captain Raich Carter proudly displays the trophy. Acknowledged as one of Sunderland's best–ever players, Carter scored the second goal in the 3 – 1 win over Preston North End. The Second World War interrupted Carter's career and when hostilities finished and football recommenced in 1946 Carter was a Derby County player whose team won the first post-war FA Cup Final against Charlton Athletic. In Hendon, Sunderland, today can be found the Raich Carter Sports Centre, a lasting tribute to a truly great Sunderland player.

Horatio Stratton Carter:

SAFC 278 Apps   128 g

Quiz 1

Monty's True or False Tester

(Answers on p 127)

1   Newcastle United once had official colours of red and white.

2   There's a team in Uruguay called Nancy Boys' Athletic.

3   The first ever Cup Final to be televised was Sunderland v PNE in 1937.

4   Sheffield United once had a 22 stone goalkeeper.

5   Rochdale once beat Man United in a league game.

6   Forfar Athletic's nickname is The Loons.

7   West Ham United used to be called Ham Ironopolis.

8   Wimbledon and Middlesbrough have both won the FA Amateur Cup.

9   Berwick Rangers once played – for two seasons – in Div 3 (North).

10 Goalnets were invented by a Whitby fisherman.

11 The first African to play in English football was Adabele Umpopo.

12 At Bury's ground there's a Cemetery End.

13 Sir Stanley Matthews was never booked in his entire career.

14 Hamburg of the Bundesliga once had a forward called Willi Winki.

15 SKY's Chris Kamara was the first professional footballer to be prosecuted for on field violence.

16 Crewe Alexandra are named after Queen Victoria's daughter.

17 Sunderland have played Morpeth Harriers and Redcar in the FA Cup.

18 In the mid-1970s Stockport's away strip was purple and yellow stripes with red shorts.

19 Barnsley once had a half-back line of Short, Sharp and Swift.

20 Grimsby Town's pre-war nickname was 'The Codpieces'.

I have many happy memories of working at Sunderland for Roker Radio over the years, here are two, both of which involve Roker Park.

In season 1996/97 Sunderland had just been promoted to the Premiership and in the fifth game of the season were playing West Ham at home on a Sunday. As you probably know, the managers have to hand in team sheets to the referee an hour before kick-off and this was the occasion when I would be given a team sheet too for making the announcements. On this particular day Graham Poll was referee and Peter Reid had already handed in the Sunderland team sheet. At about a minute past three there was still no sign of West Ham manager Harry Redknapp's team sheet, so a member of the youth team was sent along to the away dressing room to hurry it along. Another five long minutes passed (remember a team could be fined for being late) when the dressing room door burst open and Harry Redknapp came sprinting down the corridor clutching the team sheet which he gave to the ref saying, 'Sorry about that, but it's all our foreign players and I can't spell their names.' And with a team containing Dumitrescu, Bilic, Futre and Miklosko you could see his problem.

On another occasion, I can't remember the exact game, I was doing the half-time lottery on the pitch at Roker where Jimmy McNab the ex-Sunderland player was performing the draw. He drew the winning tickets at which point I would announce, 'Make yourself known to the nearest steward and come and collect your prize' which would then be presented on the pitch with photographs taken and so on.   On this day however it was snowing/sleeting quite badly and as Jimmy was wearing only a grey suit, I suggested to him that he waited in the tunnel rather than get soaked. He readily concurred and quickly began to make his way to shelter, but was stopped dead in his tracks with a look of horror on his face as I announced to the 20,000 present, 'And thanks ladies and gentlemen to Jimmy Montgomery.' He never let me forget that faux-pas and whenever I met him afterwards he would always ask without fail, 'Remember my name Bill?'

Sun. Sept. 8th 1996   Att.18,642   Roker Park   Premiership
Sunderland 0 v 0 West Ham United
Coton, Kubicki, Scott, Bracewell, Ball, Melville, Gray, Ord,
Agnew, Stewart, Quinn. Sub used: Russell.

I support a good team   Rob Mason

(Editor of the Sunderland match programme)

Sunderland won 7-1 the first time I saw them play. I went home thinking I support a good team…and waited twenty years to see them score as many in a game again!

I was nine when my Dad took me to see an FA Cup 4th Round game against Peterborough United on February 18th 1967. We were 4-0 up in 27 minutes and when we got a penalty when we were 5-0 up, Jim Baxter stepped up to take it at the Roker End.

I'd been standing in the old children's enclosure just behind the goal where my dad had put me before going into the adult section and standing just the other side of the fence behind me that separated the children's enclosure with the rest of the end.

As soon as the penalty was given I dashed to stand right behind the net. Slim Jim was putting the ball on the spot and, feeling sorry for the overworked goalie, pointed to where he was going to put it. Sure enough the 'keeper, thinking he was being conned, dived to the opposite side of the goal as Baxter stroked the ball into the corner he'd pointed out. As the forlorn 'keeper stood up, Jim looked at him and simply shrugged his shoulders as if to say 'I gave you a chance'.

All seven goals were scored by Scots that day. Neil Martin got a hat-trick, Bobby Kerr got two and John O'Hare added to Baxter's 'penna'.

I'd been to a few youth and reserve games with my Dad before that but the Peterborough cup tie was my wonderful 'debut' with the first team. Three years later I saw my first away game in a goalless night match at Carlisle. Surpassing even Monty, I made my 1000th 'appearance' against the Mags some years ago and am still going strong but I had the advantage of that great start hooking me from day one. My brother Gordon, however, saw us lose 1-0 at home to an Oxford team including Ron Atkinson in 1970 and yet he's just as keen as me. Now that's dedication!

Sat. Feb 18th 1967   Att. 43,998   Roker Park   FA Cup Round 4
Sunderland 7 v 1 Peterborough United
(O'Hare, Martin3, Kerr 2, Baxter [pen])
Montgomery, Irwin, Harvey, Todd, Kinnell, Baxter, Kerr, O'Hare,
Martin, Herd, Mulhall.

I suppose most of us are grateful to that one person who first took us to a game or inspired our love for a football team. In my case it was my mum. My father died when I was only 4 and so it was my mum who bought me my first Sunderland shirt, took me to my first game and who bought me a season ticket every single year until I left school.

When I moved to London, then Leeds and eventually Harrogate it was my mother who faithfully posted me the *Football Echo*, queued up for tickets and sent me all the latest news. She it was who began, encouraged and nurtured my love and passion for Sunderland AFC.

She moved from Sunderland to be near us, yet after only a short time in Harrogate she developed cancer and had to move in to live with us so we were able to look after her properly. She died early on Boxing Day morning in 1999.

My daughter Sarah and myself couldn't bear to be in the house whilst my mum lay dead upstairs and as we had tickets for the game at Everton we decided to travel to Liverpool to watch the match. Many people might find this a bit callous and disrespectful but I'm certain its what my mum would have wanted and on that sombre journey westwards we were able to talk about her life and how special she was to us, and watching Sunderland play that day seemed to bring us closer to her.

We lost 5-0 (I doubt I could have cheered even had we scored) and it snowed heavily on the way back, yet somehow it was fitting that the love for the club she had created should continue as a tribute to her memory.

Sun. Dec. 26th 1999   Att. 40,017   Goodison Park   Premiership

Everton 5 v 0 Sunderland

Sorensen, Makin, Bould, Butler, Gray, Schwarz, McCann, Roy, Summerbee, Quinn, Kilbane. Subs used: Williams. Reddy

1973 and all that...

By Dave Bowman

(Dave Bowman is chairman of Greater Manchester SAFCSA)

In 1973, I was working as a journalist on the Sunderland Echo sports desk and what a year it turned out to be.

It may seem like ancient history to younger SAFC fans, but to those of us who were around at the time that historic FA Cup triumph feels just like yesterday...and the memories will live forever.

I wasn't covering Sunderland at the time, but I was involved in the day to day production of the Echo sports pages and the Football Echo and my little claim to fame was that I penned that immortal and much-loved headline: "THEY'VE DONE IT!"

The famous Cup-winning Footy Echo front page ended up on cards, t-shirts and the paper is no doubt still in many a Wearside attic or cupboard. But what most people don't realise is that because of the archaic "hot metal" newspaper production system at the time, the main 'white on black' line for the Wembley day Echo had to be sent to the composing room the day before.

So as well as "THEY'VE DONE IT!" two other headlines - "HARD LUCK, LADS!" and "EXTRA AGONY AT WEMBLEY" (in the event of extra time) were also ready and waiting to be slotted into the front page.

Thankfully, of course, it was "THEY'VE DONE IT!" that was actually used and the rest as they say is history.

An estimated one million people welcomed the Cup Winners back to the North East with the famous old trophy and, quite simply, the region has seen nothing like it since.

The Wearside public's very special passion for SAFC was plain for all to see even before Cup Final day of course as anyone who witnessed those marvellous victories over high-flying Manchester City and Arsenal will testify.

The homes and shops of Sunderland and the outlying pit villages (always the bedrock of SAFC's support) were bedecked in red and white. So much so that when I moved to Manchester later the same year to work on a national newspaper that great city seemed like an alien planet by comparison.

Perhaps it is because Manchester is a city divided in football terms, but in my early days there it always astonished me that the place wasn't either decorated in red or sky blue when City or United won some trophy or other.

More likely it was because winning trophies in Manchester was not as rare an occurrence as it has turned out to be for long-suffering Sunderland fans.

But back to Wembley '73 and the sheer emotion, passion and tension of it all will be remembered forever by those who were lucky enough to be there.

Because the Lads were the rank outsiders and therefore attracted the support of the "neutrals" in the 100,000 crowd and because many fans obtained their tickets from all over the UK and beyond, Wembley that day was a sea of red and white, apart from a smallish Leeds enclave at the tunnel end of the stadium.

Back in '73, the Echo played a part in helping a few Cup-crazy fans get their hands on tickets for the big day. What happened was that as news of Wearside Cup fever spread around the country via newspapers and quirky little TV features, some people who had acquired tickets via their county FA, referee's association or football club decided to forward them on to 'real' Sunderland supporters who were finding the tickets impossible to buy.

So a number of non-committed fans from around Britain asked the

Echo to find a "good home" for the tickets - usually requesting that they went to, for example, a retired miner; deprived children or simply a lifelong fan who had been unable to get their hands on a ticket from the club's paltry allocation.

We are not talking huge numbers here, but about 10 to 15 tickets passed through the old Echo office adjacent to the Wear Bridge - and all of them went to the deserving fans the donors intended them to go to.

Contacting the lucky recipients was like being the man from Littlewoods who rang to say you had won a fortune on the pools! In truth though, most of us who were part of that vast Red & White Army on 5/5/73 thought Sunderland were just there to make up the numbers against the hottest favourites in post-war history.

So when the final whistle sounded and Bob Stokoe raced across the Wembley turf to embrace goalkeeping hero Jimmy Montgomery, there was barely a dry eye in the house as tears of emotion and joy flowed in equal measure.

Leaving the stadium and trooping down Wembley Way towards the Tube station and the coaches seemed like an anti-climax for the simple reason that everyone with red and white blood in their veins was physically and emotionally drained after kicking every ball with the Lads for the full match.

Yes, Wembley was fantastic but there wasn't an SAFC fan around who didn't say to themselves afterwards: "I wish I was back in Sunderland."

The atmosphere in the town that night was captured for posterity in a memorable Tyne Tees TV production *Meanwhile back in Sunderland.*

In 1973, Wembley echoed to the sounds of that passionate and raucous soccer anthem 'You'll never walk alone' as the Red & White Army tasted success for the first time in two generations.

Let's hope it is not too long before we all have something special to sing about again. And I don't just mean promotion to our rightful place in English football's top flight!

Sat. May 5th 1973   Att. 100,000   Wembley   FA Cup Final
Sunderland 1 v 0 Leeds United
(Porterfield)
Montgomery, Malone, Guthrie, Horswill, Pitt, Watson, Kerr, Hughes, Halom, Porterfield, Tueart. Unused sub: Young.

Almost a Hero   Jerome Hanratty, Tynemouth

When Kevin Phillips outscored everyone else in the season 1999-2000, it was the first time for 50 years that a Sunderland player had become the division's leading striker. So who held that honour half a century ago? And why did that season (1949-50) end in heartbreak, with disappointment centring on that same leading scorer and on one end-of season game?

Towards the end of the war, as we began to look forward to the restart of League football, talk was going around about a promising young man from Birmingham who was scoring lots of goals in the Midlands. As a 17 year old he had signed for Sunderland way back in 1939, but no-one up here had ever seen him. His name was Dicky Davis.

Initially, he didn't find it too easy to break into the side, but by the 1949/50 season he was the main striker in an attractive Sunderland team that was playing the best attacking football in the country and had the highest total of goals (83) in the First Division. Tall, fair-headed and thickset, he fitted perfectly the stereotype of the 'big bustling centre forward'; brave, direct, good with his head, a powerful shot, but not a lot of subtlety. Jammed up near the corner flag in a 62,000 crowd relishing a 6-0 defeat of Huddersfield, I watched in amazement as he rushed in to head the ball – with his eyes closed! He scored a lot of goals this way and none more frequently than in that season when, with only six games to go, he was the leading scorer (26 league and cup goals out of 35 matches) in a Sunderland team riding on top and well on course for that most glittering prize, the top League Championship.

Then he was injured. In his absence we lost three games in a row, including what looked a home banker – against bottom of the table Manchester City. That was probably the game that cost us the Championship. Davis returned for the final fixture to score a brace and become the League's leading goal scorer, but it was all too late and we finished third, a point behind Portsmouth who shaded Wolves on goal average.

Still, there was always next season – and Sunderland showed they meant business by signing Trevor Ford from Aston Villa for a record £30,000. I travelled 150 miles to see his home start against Sheffield Wednesday as he signed himself in with three goals and a dislodged Fulwell End goalpost. Such feats were not often to be repeated. Although Ford himself maintained a good personal record he did not seem to gel with the others. Team results suffered, while Dicky Davis sat and watched. Our former leading scorer stuck with the club for another three seasons but never had a sustained run and the end of 1953 he left the big-time for Darlington (as co-incidentally did Ford at the same time – for Cardiff.)
Sometimes gilding the lily works. In this case it didn't. However with substitution and the squad system, times have changed and present-day clubs do use duplication. After all, suppose Trevor Ford had been available to come in for that Manchester City game?

(This memory first appeared in '*Sex and Chocolate*')

Learning the Ropes   Bob Murray CBE, Chairman
SAFC

My first match was against Wolves in September 1954. It was a goalless draw but I loved every minute and was hooked from that moment onwards. I went in the Clockstand Paddock with my Dad. He had made one of those little steps on two ropes for me. They were a familiar sight at Roker Park. You hooked the ropes over the railings at the front and stood on the step so you could see the game. They were great providing you were there early enough to get a place at the front. I'm pleased to say that everyone has a good seat at the Stadium of Light these days.

Wolves were the champions and had a great team then, led by Billy Wright, the England captain. At the end of my first season Sunderland, Wolves and Portsmouth finished level on 48 points, behind the winners, Chelsea. Sunderland got to the semi-final of the FA Cup that season as well and had players like Shack, a young Stan Anderson and Billy Bingham. Shack wasn't playing at my first game but he was the first player to really make a big impression on my and I remember clearly his last ever match which was on the opening day of the 1957-58 season when he was injured against Arsenal.

Being a Sunderland supporter is part of your birthright of course and like everyone who supports the Lads, being red and white is in the blood.

Sat. Sept 15th 1954   Att. 46,463   Roker Park   Division 1
Sunderland 0 v 0 Wolves
Fraser, Hedley, McDonald, Anderson, Daniel, Elliot, Bingham, Shackleton, Purdon, Chisholm, McSeveney.

The North-East Supporter

(An edited version from 'Speke from the Harbour' an Everton fanzine)

I hate Newcastle United. I'm not sure exactly why – it could be the way their fans, stewards and police treat the visiting fans year after year. Then again it could be the way they sing their own praises, telling us all what a big club it is. Perhaps it's their arrogance based on ....well it certainly isn't based on the trophies they have won. Maybe it's the way the directors slagged off the fans, who moaned for a day or two but then had them back in the directors' box before you could say 'dog'. I would dearly love to see Newcastle back in the second tier where they belong.

I like Sunderland. Their fans are loyal like ours, not idiotic caricatures like the Geordies. They've a lovely new shiny ground with a good atmosphere. They don't sing their own praises and have won a trophy within living memory. With their rich history they belong in the Premier League and their stand at Roker had the same type of criss-cross ironwork as our stand at Goodison.

The Wingate Bus   George Davies

Chairman, Wingate Branch, SAFCSA

Eric Gates was amazed by it, he loved it. He should have done, it's provided him with enough humorous ammunition over the years.

It all started in the 80s. The membership of the Wingate Branch of the SAFCSA was rising and even though a ticket for the game was about £2 and travel to away games on a British Rail Awayday was probably around a massive £3.75½p. (Yes, Decimalisation had occurred) The Committee of the

Wingate Branch of the SAFCSA decided it would be a good idea to save money for the Wingate masses and buy a bus. Off we went cash in hand (around £1500.62½p) down to Roberts.

There it was! Roberts didn't need to sell it to us, it sold itself : not much rust, Road Tax current, only one flat tyre, a Bedford Bus (55 seats, some ripped) - Transport Heaven. We haggled furiously. We started at £1400, he started at £1500.62½p.

Yeeeeeessssssssss! we'd done it. The start of a long and happy era had begun; the haggling had paid off...... we got it for £1500.60p CHEAP TRANSPORT FOR ALL!!!

Triumphant, Mick, Dave and Dave were recapping our successful day; we were picking the bus up on Tuesday. "Who's gonna pick it up?" said Dave B.

"Who's got a bus licence?" said Dave F.

"Bugger!"

"Never mind, what's the biggest thing anyone's got a licence for?" said Mick. "That'll do."

Travelling to and from games was great, loads of atmosphere on the bus and of course loads of beer. Weekend after weekend we sped to games cruising at 57mph (on the flat) scarves, arms and legs hanging out of the windows. Every one used to pass us waving, smiles on their faces, you could see them wondering how the Hell we were going to get there.

But we did get there, every time! Before lunchtime as well, and sometimes before some of those smiling faces, which, of course when they saw us their expressions had turned to those of disbelief. One day Gatesy was standing outside of one of the London grounds (which one it was escapes me) but when the first lad got off the bus Gatesy remarked, "You haven't travelled all this way in that heap of sh*te have you?" Then some of the bigger lads disembarked - "Nice bus lads!" Gatesy commented.

It wasn't all smiles at a breakneck speed though, for there were times when things did get a bit rough. Driving down to a game against Tottenham, the driver was hanging over the steering wheel to see through driving snow when we were stopped by the police somewhere near Nottingham. "You'll have to turn round the roads are blocked with snow!" Well the QE2 had a smaller turning circle than our Bedford Bus and we had to reverse 2 miles to get to a point where we could turn round, with one unfortunate passenger having to direct the driver backwards from the outside with a blizzard full in his face, visibility was that bad.

Another Winter's Tale was born when we were travelling to one away game. The temperature outside was well into the minuses and blow me just after we set off the heating died on the bus. You'd have thought we were Chelsea supporters 'cos we were all blue by the time we got to Wetherby, when luckily the heating started working again.

Man Utd fans are a generous sort. We were leaving Old Trafford (guess what? in the middle of winter again) and one of them decided to lend us a brick for our journey, delivered through the back window of course. Being bloody cold outside, our unexpected gift had its shortfalls. The extra (permanent) ventilation that it had it had provided during delivery was causing problems for the fan next to the window so it was decided that every one should have their turn to catch hypothermia on a rotational basis. We still have the brick and hope to return it sometime.

Teamwork is the essence of the branch as we found out on a trip to Stoke City. When we stopped everyone was looking out of the window for a toilet or a Café or Bar……..Nothing, then the driver said, "Everybody Out!"

Fans "????????????"

Driver, "We've ran out of Diesel! You're gonna have to push. It's only quarter of a mile to the next services." He didn't seem too phased about it, but of course he didn't have to push 4 tons of Bedford Bus.

I could go on, but we'll leave it there with a few of the tales of the Wingate bus which has become a bit of local folklore and even mentioned during match day commentaries on local radio.

Sadly we no longer have a bus, it was costing a fortune in running costs and frostbite treatments for the members.

We had to sell it, not a popular decision. At £1500 we thought it was a bargain for someone, the trouble is 'someone' didn't turn up and we ended up flogging it to a bus company for £650 who only wanted the rear axle, the rest of it going to that immortal scrap yard in the sky.

The memories about the bus still linger on within the branch and we reflect often about our wonderful Bedford over a beer and are comforted to know that part of it still lives, breaking down occasionally and brightening up other people's lives.

Lynn's Lists

Tom Lynn, East Herrington

I have followed SAFC regularly since the late 60s and the friend of my Dad's who first took me to Roker Park most weeks, Keith Richardson, recently sadly passed away. He has a lot to answer for. If not for him I might be a well-balanced individual instead of the emotionally challenged wreck that following The Lads has turned me into. Sunderland 'til I Die? Not much choice now, eh?

Top Dozen Games Seen [No particular order].

1. Sunderland 3-1 Man City - FA Cup 5th Round Replay, 1973.
    Roker Park was never louder than it was that night.

2. Sunderland 2-1 Arsenal - FA Cup Semi-Final, 1973.
    Pit yackers, shipyard lads and most fans there cried at the final whistle.

3. Sunderland 4-1 Chelsea - Premiership, 1999-2000.
    The best pure footballing display I've witnessed from a Sunderland team.

4. Newcastle Utd 1-2 Sunderland - Premiership, 2000-2001.
    Sorensen's penalty save preceded a night of delirium around the city centre.

5. Chelsea 2-3 Sunderland - Milk Cup Semi-Final Second Leg, 1985.
    Colin West slotting the ball in, with a Police horse in the penalty area.

6. Sunderland 2-2 Newcastle Utd - Premiership, 1999-2000.
    0-2 down, SuperKev equalized to the biggest din the SoL has witnessed.

7.   Newcastle Utd 0-2 Sunderland - Play Off Semi-Final second leg, 1989-90.

You should have seen the Gallowgate End when Marco's goal went in!

8.   Sunderland 1-0 Leeds United - FA Cup Final 1973.

Porterfield. 1-0. The most emotional FA Cup Final of all time and I was there.

9.   Sunderland 2-0 West Ham United - Old Second Division, 1979-80.

Clinched promotion over that year's FA Cup Winners. 47,000 with 15,000 outside.

10.   Sunderland 1-0 Newcastle Utd - Old Second Division, 1979-80.

Stan Cummins sent Wearside mental with his winner at the Fulwell End.

11.   Man United 3-2 Sunderland - Old Second Division, 1974-75.

63,000 saw the game voted 'Game of the Season' by Match of the Day viewers.

12.   Newcastle Utd 1-4 Sunderland - Old Second Division, 1978-79.

Got bitten by a Police dog before the game. "So what?" Rowell scored a hat-trick!

10 Most Memorable Goals

1. PORTERFIELD v Leeds - FA Cup Final, 1973 [How mental did we go?]

2. PHILLIPS v Chelsea [h] - Premiership, 1999-2000 [25 yard screamer]

3. GABBIADINI v Newcastle [a] - Play-Off semi second leg, 1990 [Yessss!!!!!]

4. HAWLEY v Arsenal [h] - Old First Division, 1980-81 [beat Pat Jennings from just inside his own half]

5. ARMSTRONG v Chelsea [h] - FA Cup 6th Round, 1992 [Roker went crazy]

6. HALOM v Man City - FA Cup 5th Round Replay, 1973 [Fabulous angled volley]

7. PHILLIPS v Newcastle [h] - Premiership, 1999-2000 [Equaliser after being 0-2 down - the BBC microphones behind the North Stand goal exploded!]

8. QUINN v Newcastle [a] - Premiership, 2000-01 [Pick that out, Shay!]

9. PHILLIPS v Newcastle [a] - Premiership, 1999-2000 [Singing In The Rain!]

10. HUGHES v Arsenal - FA Cup Semi-Final, 1973 [People went berserk!]

Best Sunderland X1 from players I've seen

[4-3-3 formation]

Jim Montgomery

Chris Makin   Dave Watson   Steve Bould   Joe Bolton

Nicky Summerbee   Tony Towers   Stefan Schwarz

Bryan 'Pop' Robson   Niall Quinn   Kevin Phillips.

TOP 10 SAFC 'CHARACTERS'

JOE BOLTON [Birtley's finest-hard as nails on and off the pitch]

BILLY WHITEHURST [Marco's minder for a while. Genuine hard man]

JOHN KAY [Remember him 'rowing' off the pitch after breaking his leg!]

FRANK WORTHINGTON [Wine, women, song…oh yeah, and football!]

JIM BAXTER [Still a drinking legend amongst older Wearsiders!]

CHARLIE HURLEY [Great player still idolized by thousands today]

BARRY SIDDALL [Liked a few pints and a laugh down the Saltgrass, Deptford]

VIC HALOM [Barrel-chested legend of the 1973 FA Cup run - liked a good time!]

KEVIN BALL [Admits Sunderland-born Mick Harford was his hardest opponent]

EMERSON THOME [Top bloke, once served behind the bar in Idols in Sunderland City Centre as fans came back from the 2-1 win at Newcastle in November, 2000 - he knew what it meant to us all]

THEY LIVED THE DREAM

- A team of North Easterners who played for The Lads.

Jim Montgomery   [Southwick]

Warney Cresswell   [South Shields]

Colin Todd   [Chester le Street]

Stan Anderson   [Horden]

Mickey Gray   [Castletown]

Len Duns   [Newcastle]

Gary Rowell   [Seaham]

Don Hutchison   [Gateshead]

Chris Waddle   [Heworth]

Raich Carter   [Hendon]

Bobby Gurney   [Silksworth]

Port and Lemon   Terry Coward, Hartlepool

In the mid 80s the youth team were playing in the FA Youth Cup at Hartlepool, which is my home town, so naturally I went along. Only the 'main' stand was open so everyone was tightly packed in with the icy wind from the North Sea biting into our faces. My mate was on my right and some other bloke who I didn't know on my left.

As we settled into the game, in front of us, slightly to the right, we noticed other non-playing members of the Sunderland Youth Squad including Paul Lemon who was not playing because he'd recently become a regular first team player. Recognising him, my mate and I then went on to discuss in no uncertain terms how the unfortunately named Lemon was absolutely useless and would never be a future success given all his obvious limitations.

When half time arrived Paul Lemon and the other youth team players got to their feet to make their way to the tea bar. Suddenly Paul Lemon turned round, looked in our direction and shouted to the bloke on my left, "Do you want a cup of tea…..DAD!"

An Ugly Incident   Paul and Andrea Tindle, Pannal

We've never forgotten this event from an away game at Middlesbrough in the late nineties. We were looking for our seats when a Sunderland supporter in front of us saw one of his friends seated in the row ahead.

He called out, "Hi Jimmy are ye alright? Is that your lass with you?"

"Fine. Yeah it's our lass," came the reply.

At which the first supporter said, "God she's an ugly bugger."

Almost the whole stand turned to look at the poor girl sitting there and it had to be said the supporter wasn't totally wrong.

I used to help run a local football club called the Billingham Swan. My favourite position was in goal and to be honest I wasn't that good. Well one Sunday morning we must have been short of players because "Ray the Cat" got the nod.

During the match our right back Colin Burnett was running down the wing with the striker breathing down his neck. "Away! Away!" I shouted (always wanting to take the easy option) but Colin duly passed the ball back to me, which I picked up. Now the new pass back rule had just been implemented and I had forgotten about it which meant a free kick was given right on the penalty spot.

After the grief from my fellow players died down they asked "Ray where do you want us?"

"All 10 of you on the line I'll stand in front of you and attack the ball."

"Are you sure?" came their reply.

"Don't worry," said I. "I once saw Barry Siddall do it for Sunderland." So we all lined up eagerly, the free kick was taken and BANGED right in the top corner for a goal. All my team mates just glared at me shaking their heads. I glared back and retorted, "Never mind lads Siddall never saved it either."

I am sure that we have all had situations at away games when you have just been in the wrong place at the wrong time with the possibility of ending up the wrong side of a black eye! Well my situation was born more out of stupidity rather than bad luck…..

Going back to the 1996-7 season when we were playing the Smoggies at the Riverside, Shaun (my nephew) was living in Billingham. As we couldn't get tickets for the Sunderland end, we decided to chance our arm and see if we could pick up a couple outside the ground. His local ran a bus to and from games and as I had been in there a couple of times before and the natives seemed pretty friendly, we decided to take advantage of the hospitality. We arrived at the pub just after opening time and everything seemed fine, the Carling was going down nicely and the small crowd already in didn't seem to be bothered we were Mackems. As the pub started to fill, I sensed the atmosphere start to change and noticed a pretty mean squad of locals starting to give us the eye. By about half an hour before we were to hop onto the bus I am sure that half of the Boro 'Front Line' had been tipped off we were in – and the atmosphere was changing by the minute! Being the born coward I am, I would have been more than happy to slip out of the back door and make a run for it – but Shaun, by now having had his 6 pint pre-match aperitif, and more importantly having paid his 50p for the bus was having none of it!

The bus duly arrived and everybody started to congregate in order to board – the Boro lads by this time were enthusiastically making 'cut-throat' signs at us. Shaun responded in his usual manner by taking his coat off and proudly displaying his Sunderland shirt – which for some reason they didn't see the funny side of.

We all boarded without any physical violence but plenty of taunts of what they were going to do to us when we got to the ground. We managed to grab a couple of seats downstairs with most of the Neanderthals going up stairs. The ride lasted about 20 minutes (ish) but seemed at least 3 hours. After a couple of renditions of "You are going to get your fxxxxx heads kicked in", "Die Mackems Die" and "You're going home by fxxxxxx ambulance" they finally settled down and serenaded us the rest of the way with "Get the Mackems off the bus" (in time with the stomping of their feet).

As we neared the ground we could see plenty of Sunderland fans milling about in smallish groups so we did have a glimmer of hope that we could make a run for it once the bus stopped. This idea was quickly thwarted however when some of the choir came downstairs and blocked our exit. By this time the effects of the alcohol were quickly wearing off and I was close to parting with some brown adrenaline but as it would slow down my escape I thought the better of it! As the bus started to slow to a stop I could see a large group of 'boys' surrounded by a police video surveillance team walking slowly towards the ground. The Boro lads on the bus by now were getting pretty restless, Shaun was picking his target and I was asking for divine intervention. With a jolt, the bus pulled up sharply due to the 'boys' outside and the police having a difference of opinion which they were settling without recourse to the Queensbury rules. The next thing I knew was Shaun jumping up and down like a demented banshee shouting, "They're the Casuals!" The look on the faces of the 'Boro lads' was a picture! As the bus could get no further they had to get off and funnily enough they didn't wait around long enough to have their chat with us as promised, and were last seen being chased down the road by a group of equally fiercesome Seaburn Casuals!

Yes, we did have a little swagger in our step walking to the ground, but then it is not every day you survive a ride with a bus load of Boro' nutters!

Definitely a day I won't forget……..

P.S We did get tickets (although in with the home fans); we won 1-0 and decided to get a taxi back!

Sat. April 19th 1997   Att. 30,106   Riverside   Premiership
Middlesbrough 0 v 1 Sunderland
(Williams)
Perez, Hall, M Gray, Ball, Ord, Bracewell, Williams. Waddle,
Johnston, Quinn, Howey. Subs used: Russell, Rae.

Training insults   Niall Quinn

One morning at Charlie Hurley's training centre a young blind kid from Hendon came to visit the players.

He was a terrific child and engaged in stern conversation with all of our group. He recognised each player he was talking to by their accents and didn't hold back on his feelings on us not yet being in the Premiership.

To say he was cheeky would be kind to him but he was great craic. The highlight came when our captain Michael Gray enquired whether he was a Sunderland fan or a Newcastle fan such was the stick he was unloading on the players. I'll never forget his answer, "If ye had a scored the effing penalty ye soft twat I would not have to be giving out to yez."

Quiz 2

Monty's Find the Pairs

Match the Sunderland player or manager with one of the objects from the right hand column.

(Answers on p 127)

Kevin Phillips	a dog
Peter Reid	The Roker Hotel
Laurie McMenemy	a trilby
John Kay	Guinness
Julio Arca	Elvis Presley
Jason McAteer	an arrow
Freddie Shepherd	a white handkerchief
Martin Smith	an autobiography
Bob Stokoe	a tractor
Len Shackleton	a cricket bat
Craig Russell	a painting
Niall Quinn	a blank page
Jody Craddock	a yard dog scrapper
Willie Watson	Pele's son
Jim Baxter	a jellyfish

Billingham and its surrounding districts, situated about 3 miles to the north of the River Tees have always had a strong Sunderland following. Indeed, the area once belonged to County Durham before some politician invented Cleveland and the Teesside conurbation grew bigger and smoggier. However, tradition in many families remains strong and other more recent native County Durhamers have moved into the area to find work.

There wasn't an official supporters' branch formed however until the weeks leading up to the play off final in 1998. Many people were looking out for ways to get to the match and the first meeting was held in the Billingham Arms Hotel, mainly to organise this transport. Despite the disappointment of the final, many supporters elected to carry the meetings on and the second was held a month later in the Travellers Rest public house in Hartlepool when over 70 supporters attended. A committee was elected and the Billingham & District Branch became the 25th official SAFC Supporters Association branch.

Over the next few years we've grown from strength to strength-boasting over 160 members by the middle of 1999. A branch newsletter aptly named 'The A19' was produced and meetings were held on a monthly basis. Many successful functions have taken place including barbeques, a pig racing night, Christmas parties, promotion parties, a TWR night out, a trip to the Sunderland Greyhound track, a number of full branch away trips, a stadium tour and various quiz and games nights. A number of ex-players and football celebrities have also been invited to take part in our popular football talk-ins, including Eric Gates, Rob Mason, Chris Turner, Jimmy Montgomery, Jimmy NcNab, Richie Pitt and George Tyson.

There are now over 300 season ticket holders in the Billingham area alone, so scope for increasing membership is constantly growing and the smoggies certainly know that we are here. The branch has also raised well over £6000 for various charities since its inception in 1998. The beneficiaries have included a local Cystic Fibrosis charity, the Anthony Nolan Bone Marrow Trust, the British Heart Foundation and the British Alzheimer's Society.

Most of the charity monies have been raised via supporters taking part in our now annual Red 'n' White March to the Stadium of Light. Over 50 members make the 32-mile trek each April and this has proved massively enjoyable and successful. Our charity walk has now become a very popular event and up to 2005, we have raised £25,000 for charities spreading the range of chosen charities including local Sunderland charities as the good people of Sunderland generously contribute and even children's charities in Middlesbrough proving that when it comes to good causes we can set our football loyalties aside.

A big thank you has to go CENTURY FM Radio and particularly Eric Gates (who has done the walk twice himself) for promoting the event. In 2005 Eric invited people to walk with him, the response was amazing, even Newcastle fans travelling 50 miles south just to do the walk, so much so that we had to limit the numbers. Obviously you can't just march 80 to 100 people up the A19, it is unsafe and what's more the police wouldn't allow it. So a route was mapped out and depending on kick off we start around midnight usually in the month of April, walking through the night with walkers as young as 8 years and old as 60 all successfully completing.

We take the Castle Eden Walkway, carry on through the villages of Wingate and Station Town. Then pick up the Castle Eden Walk way again, which at this part is an old mining track. This takes into Albion Pub in Ryhope a traditional stop on the way to the SOL. Here we have a well earned break, a few beers, change for the match and do the final push collecting in buckets as we go. We can raise up to £700 in the buckets such is the generosity of the Sunderland public.

We always receive a good reception from the fans as we walk through the city and at the SOL as we do a lap of the pitch. Also a special mention needs to be made to the back up team who stop up all night working ahead of the walkers, setting up rest stations, providing refreshments, First Aid and driving the mini-buses.

We are just one of the many thriving SAFC Supporters branches which offer supporters the opportunity to become more a part of Sunderland Football Club.

It's only a Game   Ken Gambles

I suppose I've never really confused the importance of football with the importance of living, and of course football is 'only a game', yet it has that astonishing ability to provide these magical, marvellous moments you'll never forget as well as plunging you into an unhappiness bordering on despair.

Over the last 41 years of watching the lads the relegations, triumphs or near misses have formed a litany most supporters can recite by heart: 1964, 1970, 1973, 1976, 1977, 1980 etc, etc. (and thank goodness we're back in the top flight) but I thought I'd try to identify three very personal and specific memories which for me proved very hard to take. It may seem illogical, immature even, to feel so down about the result of a football match, but had anyone said to me at these times, 'Come on, it's only a game', I don't think I'd have been responsible for my actions.

In 1967 Leeds United were flying high – a side packed with internationals, always competing for honours and universally disliked for their aggressive 'professionalism'. Sunderland were muddling along as usual in the lower reaches of the top flight, but FA Cup wins at home over Brentford 5-2 and Peterborough 7-1 paired us with the mighty Leeds at Roker in Round 5. The game was on 'Match of the Day', a rarity for us at this time; Bobby Kerr had his leg broken by Norman Hunter, yet we drew 1-1 and were thus expected to bow out at Elland Road in the replay. A Leeds record crowd of 57,892 crammed into the ground; there was the drama of a collapsed crush barrier and then followed an epic struggle, a terrific encounter that ended 1-1 after extra time where Sunderland were every bit as good as their illustrious opposition.

The second replay was designated for Boothferry Park, Hull on March 17 1967 in front of a sell out crowd of 40,000. Once again the Lads matched Leeds in all areas of the pitch and the game was there for the winning. Then came the moment. At 1-1 with only a minute of normal time remaining an innocuous challenge by Cec Irwin on Jimmy Greenhoff saw the Leeds striker sprawl dramatically in the box and the infamous (well he was in the sixties) Ken Stokes award a soft penalty. All hell broke loose – George Herd and George Mulhall were sent off and Mackem hearts everywhere were broken as the penalty was scored and we were out.

I can still almost feel the burning sense of injustice, anger and misery that overwhelmed me that night compounded by the fact that living in Barnsley I had to sit and fume and ache in a train full of Leeds supporters on the hour's journey back to Leeds where I then had to 'sleep' on the station until a 6.30am departure back home. (By the way that season Leeds went out in the semis to Chelsea rather controversially (thank goodness) and then of course there was the 1973 Cup Final when justice was done once and for all.)

Coincidentally heartache number two occurred at Barnsley in 1995 in the notorious 'grit storm'. We were struggling desperately to avoid the drop to the third tier again. With about 8 games left the situation looked bad as we travelled to Barnsley for a Friday night fixture. Mick Buxton as manager was proving clueless and the writing really seemed to be on the wall. Some cause for optimism (misguided it proved) came with the £600,000 signing of Brett Angell from Everton, a player who could score at will against us, but could he do the business for us? In addition Dominic Matteo was signed on loan from Liverpool (an illegal signing as it later proved, but luckily we weren't docked points for it.)

An early disallowed goal direct from a throw-in (or did Angell get the merest of touches?) raised spirits but predictably we capitulated far too easily to lose 2-0. The whole sorry situation was compounded by a strong wind blowing in our faces on the open terracing behind the goal carrying lethal amounts of grit and dust from the re-development work at the other end. I'm sure that anyone who was there won't have forgotten it. All our rivals were due to play the following day and we were surely doomed. The feelings on the journey home were those of utter despondency and pessimism and another stay in Division 3 looked horribly likely. But, Peter Reid was appointed within days, and a last minute goal from Craig Russell against Sheffield United plus a vital goal from 'son of Pele' Martin Smith against Swindon saw us manage to avoid the drop and of course in 1996 we were champions and on our way to the Premier. It was only 4 years after that most miserable of nights that we played Barnsley near the end of the season and clinched the championship again with a powerful, fluent 3-1 victory to the strains of a continuous "We're on our way, We're on our way, To the Premier' (ad infinitum)

My third particular soul-wrenching moment I'm afraid is one from that nightmarish, shameful, mentally-scarring 2002-2003 relegation season. Just about any game that season was misery-inducing and who can forget the 15 consecutive defeats, three own goals in eight minutes, the spineless capitulations and so on? The one moment for me, however, which summed up the whole sorry season and left me feeling totally lousy and chewed-up was the home game against the Boro'. As usual that season we were a goal down early on then two down by half time with little hope of recovery.

After the break however we played with a bit more spark, and Super Kev pulled one back with a wonderful strike. For once that season the whole of the SOL responded; the atmosphere was cracking, the belief growing, the stands rocking. Was this to be the turning point? No. Kevin Kilbane (of blessed memory) finding himself closed down on the halfway line decided for some inexplicable reason to play a delicately weighted back-pass – straight into the path of Boro' forward Malcolm Christie who calmly slotted home number 3. Pricked balloon, End of story, Kaput, Good Night Vienna. Totally speechless and utterly bereft we knew the game was up and that relegation was such a certainty that even the later appointed Mick McCarthy couldn't effect a turnaround and put a stop to the unforgivable dross and awful rot we put up with that season. (Perhaps we'll get our revenge on the Boro' now we're back in the Premier.) [Stop Press – we did!]

So, three very personal moments of dejection and hopelessness that even the success of the cup and promotion can't fully erase. When my daughter first wanted to come to watch the Lads with me in 1989 I told her what she could expect – some highs and plenty of lows – that's the lot of a Sunderland Supporter. She knows herself now and is a season ticket holder of 11 years standing. But as they say, the downs are character-forming, strength comes from adversity, and certainly when I think back to those times and how others 'suffered' too, we still are Sunderland, we keep the faith, we still travel all over the country (and abroad) to watch them and that's what makes us so special. Good and bad, success and failure, its all part of the package. As for football 'only being a game', well of course it is, but what a game that so profoundly stirs the emotions and gives us incredible memories. Someone once said 'Football is the most important of the unimportant things in life' and that'll do me fine.

Mon. March 20th 1967   Att. 40,456   Boothferry Park   FA Cup Round 5 (Second Replay)
Sunderland 1 v 2 Leeds United
(Gauden)
Montgomery, Irwin, Harvey, Todd, Kinnell, Baxter, Gauden, O'Hare, Martin, Herd, Mulhall.

Fri. Mar. 24th 1995   Att. 7,803   Oakwell   Division 1
Barnsley 2 v 0 Sunderland
Norman, Kubicki, Scott, Ord, Melville, M Smith, Agnew, Armstrong, Matteo, Gray, Angell. Subs used: Russell, M Gray

Sat. Feb. 22nd 2003   Att. 42,134   Stadium of Light   Premiership
Sunderland 1 v 3 Middlesbrough
(Phillips)
Sorensen, Wright, Caldwell, El Karkouri, Gray, McCann, Kilbane, Reyna, McAteer, Phillips, Flo. Subs used, Piper, Proctor, Arca.

Most football supporters will point out the merits of a good away trip. 3rd January 1998 was one of those days out where everything is just right and there is a real buzz. That is what following Sunderland AFC is like – you can be on the floor one minute and up the next. There is no such thing as a smooth ride with this club.

This trip had particular significance to me as I had been writing articles for the Rotherham United fanzine "Moulin Rouge" and it was the first time I had seen my heroes play against Rotherham.

We arrived from Sheffield around 1 o'clock and made a beeline for the Moulders Rest, the main Rotherham pub near the ground and also where the fanzine people would be found. However, we were blocked by bouncers and told that there were no away fans allowed in on this particular day. Disappointed but with no complaints we searched for somewhere to eat and settled for Reo's.

The restaurant was heaving with fans and the waiters and waitresses were running around frantically. We asked one waitress what the attendance was likely to be. She said normally it was quite small but there would obviously be a big one today. When I suggested that it could reach 6,000 she said, "No, sometimes they ring me up and I play fullback."

We moved onto Millmoor at 2.30pm and despite lots of remarks about the ground, basically we all loved the experience of standing in a shed again and moved right to the front behind Lionel Perez's goal. One of the things about modern stadiums is you can find yourself some way away from the pitch side albeit with a good view so it was nice to stand (yes stand!!) near the pitch again. The atmosphere was building up towards kick off. Eventually the teams came out and we proceeded to scare the Roth ball boys witless. I suddenly realised as soon as we had taken our positions the difference between my thoughts on the two clubs. Although I knew before, it really hit me standing on that Railway End that I was Sunderland through and through and I only had an interest in Rotherham through my fanzine connections. Just being part of that wonderful away noise really makes you think how important the club is to you and how it is the only one for you. I have lost count of the number of times I have gone though promotions and relegations or just simple fixtures like this and I have looked around at the people in the ground with me and thought how special the fans of the club are and how much being part of that means to me. It is difficult to put into words that kind of feeling that you get at these moments.

The game kicked off and the Millers gave a good account of themselves forcing Perez into some trademark "saved by frog's legs" saves. However, we looked just as threatening and sorted ourselves out from a dodgy penalty. I couldn't judge from where I was standing but on TV afterwards it looked accidental handball.

We took control of the second half when Phillips scored a classic Super Kev goal, taking strike in his stride. Just so we weren't too comfortable Rotherham scored a peach to pull it back to 2-1. Trevor Berry sold a fantastic dummy to Mickey Gray who was enjoying his best form at the time and Berry's cross was finished by the raggy-haired Darren Garner.

The Mighty Atom completed his four before the Mighty Quinn made it five. A bloke behind me on the bus the following week said he had us to win 4-1 at 25/1 so he must have been slightly cheesed off that Quinn ruined the perfect day for him!

Finally we left and nearly got crushed going through the gates with police looking on, something that I have experienced at Millmoor more times since. So a day of many twists and turns, but it was great to go home having won so handsomely. I suppose nothing out of the ordinary occurred on this trip (a 5-1 away win! Ed) but I think it sums up so many good days out and the feeling you get when you are on tour with your club and when you sing your heart out and a good result tops it off.

It's not always so straightforward though. Some away games I have had to watch on TV. Easy you might think – just find a pub and a view. This was the case earlier in the season and I've also had to race my way up the A19 to my parents' to watch games. However later on in the 2004-5 season I found that living in York meant I would find it difficult to catch the game against Wolverhampton Wanderers. I had travelled over the other side of town as the plan was to watch the game in a pub local to my friend and then go back to my friend's house for a night of beers and DVDs. It didn't quite work out that way. No, we couldn't get the football because the passion of the area was on – Super League! Yes, big blokes chasing eggs. So we had to find another pub quickly. Over the road then to The Plough. The TV wasn't on and so we politely asked if we could watch and the barman kindly turned it on for us. We settled into watching the game and Stephen Elliott scored a great goal to much celebration but unfortunately this was followed by an equaliser for Wolves, when suddenly the rugby came on! It turned out the landlord was watching it upstairs and so it came on down in the bar as well. We moaned at the barman but he said it wasn't his choice. Eventually the landlord came in the bar and apologised to us but said that he liked rugby. "So there," basically. Never mind about looking after your customers or anything.

Quickly we moved onto another pub and while waiting to be served we got some advice on where we might find the game on from someone my friend knew, so we quickly cancelled the drinks and ventured on into town to pubs on the outskirts. The first had the rugby on. Very much so. They were screaming at the screen. What was wrong with them? Where was the football?

The next pub. Again no football. We had a good pint and a chat and trudged back to my friend's house. We must have walked 2-3 miles in total but absolutely with no success. As it turned out we saw both goals in the 1-1 draw. I think this is what following Sunderland does to you. You'll do the daftest things to try and see the game, and you'll usually get a memorable night for it whatever the reasons for it.

Thankfully the 2005 Championship clinching game against West Ham was on live on a Friday in city centre pubs and I enjoyed it in the Old White Swan with a ghetto of fellow Mackems who had gathered there. That's Sunderland supporters for you. We're everywhere!

Sat. Jan 3rd 1998   Att. 10,483   Millmoor   FA Cup 3
Rotherham Utd 1 v 5 Sunderland
                        (Quinn, Phillips 4)
Perez, Holloway, Craddock, Ball, M Gray, Clark,
Johnston, Rae
Williams, Quinn, Phillips. No subs used.

No Respect   Paul Tindle, Pannal

I am a headteacher at a Leeds primary school and my love for Sunderland AFC is well known amongst the children and their parents.

One day I had to reprimand a 7 year old autistic child who had lashed out whilst playing football in the playground at break-time. I took him to one side and gently explained that football was a game to be enjoyed, that winning and losing were all part of the experience and that it was quite wrong to lash out when things weren't going your way.

Quick as a flash he shot back 'What do you know about football? You're a Sunderland Supporter!'

I must admit that over the years I've asked myself the same question.

Supermick   Steve Hart, Starbeck

This was the profile of a game Sunderland typically lose. Although five points clear at the top, we had just lost our first game of the season, against Barnsley at home. Sheffield United were on a good run, three consecutive wins. Kevin Phillips was still injured. An awkward away game if ever there was one.

But Sunderland produced their best performance of the season and one of our main promotion rivals were played off the park. It was all but over after quarter of an hour.

Summerbee was brought down on the right. He picked himself up, dusted himself down and whipped in a cross which eluded everyone except Quinn, who stooped to head in at the far post. Then, a goal by Bridges. He controlled Makin's cross into the box with his back to goal and a defender on his back. That defender was Steve Bruce, and his career was about to end. With a flick and a feint Bridges was gone, and he beat keeper Tracey with supreme coolness.

The only danger to Sunderland now was their own casualness and Sorensen had to stand tall a couple of times.

Johnston and Summerbee were elusive on the wings; Bridges and Quinn menacing up front; Clark and Ball had a tight grip in midfield; at any sniff of a threat, the door was snapped shut by Melville and Co.

The third goal; Sunderland had a free kick at left back, Johnston acted quickly and his long ball released Bridges, after it like a greyhound out of the traps. Defenders floundering in his wake, he finished after rounding Tracey.

There was lots of 'ole' football in the second half as Sunderland stroked the ball around. Makin's shot was saved by Tracey and Quinn scored from the rebound. Despite his missing of a penalty, this was the game when we knew for sure (like Steve Bruce) that Michael Bridges had a real future in the game. What a shame that over the years because of injuries he never quite lived up to his astonishing potential.

Sat. Nov 28th 1998   Att. 25,229   Bramall Lane   Division 1
Sheffield United 0 v 4 Sunderland
(Bridges 2, Quinn 2)
Sorensen, Scott, Butler, Melville, Makin. Clark, Johnston, Ball, Quinn, Bridges, Summerbee. Subs used, Craddock, Dichio, McCann.

An Outsider Looking In

Graeme Garvey, Leeds Fan

A Sunderland supporter is an optipessimist. He or she is someone who always fears the worst but continues to turn up in the hope that, this time, it might just turn out all right.

I've met a good number of Sunderland fans. They seem a nice bunch generally – fair-minded, good-humoured, sporting. All you'd expect from true football supporters. Until, that is, mention is made of The Mags. Then reason and charity fly out of the window. Imagine if Newcastle had been successful. No don't.

I've seen quite a few Sunderland games over the years, one way and another. This is mainly because a mate is a supporter who doesn't drive. I don't come from Wearside but I understand quite a lot of what the fans say and I've found the pub and terrace wit really enjoyable. Can't say the same for the 'red –plastic-seat-like-buckets wit' but that's another matter.

And in all the talk I've heard and understood, the one word I would never use to describe Sunderland fans is cocky. They can't afford to be. They live in the real world, a world where the worst happens. Which topic is likely to stir the greater debate, the best Sunderland team ever, or the worst? Exactly.

Remember when Sunderland needed to win their last 3 matches to stay up? Which particular season you ask? Just to jog your memories (sorry, but it's worth it in the end) it was in 1986. We drove up to Roker on a fine, early summer's evening. It could have been Ice Station Zebra for the mood in the town before kick-off.

We entered the Pilot Cutter (now Harbour View) to find the lads already assembled. Well, you've got to get some fun out of the evening. I'd driven my mate up because it meant so much to him. They knew it and were deeply grateful for my turning up to bear witness. "Good of you to come," one said in hushed tones, the only time I'd ever heard that said outside of a funeral.

I felt like replying, "Sorry for your trouble."

Amidst all the tension there was plenty of laughter, even if some of it verged on hysteria, and we left the pub on a rising tide of anxious hope, joining the red and white throng on their way to see the final act of the tragedy.

Of course, Sunderland beat Shrewsbury 2-0 and defied the odds by winning the final game v Stoke City to stay up.

They went down the next season, of course.

Well, what would you expect, being an optipessimist?

Tues. April 29th 1986   Att. 15,507   Roker Park   Division 2
Sunderland 2 v 0 Shrewsbury Town
(Gates, Proctor)
Dibble, Venison, Kennedy, Gray, Bennett, Elliot, Ford, Gayle,
Wallace, Gates, Proctor.

The Day Bob Laughed   Kelvin Powell

The moment Gordon Armstrong's header hit the back of the net late on in the quarter-final replay against Chelsea, thoughts of the semi-final became uppermost in my mind. Everything else in life seemed to take second place. The date was set. Sunday April 4, the venue Hillsborough, our opponents Norwich.

In February, the company I work for had invited the wife and I down to London for a theatre evening followed by dinner and a stay-over at a plush hotel in the West End on Saturday April 3. My wife was really looking forward to it and had even splashed out on a new outfit. As soon as she found out that Sunderland were to play Norwich on the fourth, she told me there was a problem because we would be in London the night before and that out three children needed to be picked up from their grandmother in Gloucestershire, some 100 miles away, before we could return home.

It seemed an impossible situation and I told my wife I was sorry but we would not be going to London. Things had to be put into perspective and order of importance. The kids and their grandmother had been looking forward to seeing each other and my wife, well words could not describe her disappointment. There was hell on. I thought 'She'll get over it. I'll find a way to make things up' and started by buying her a big bunch of flowers. It wasn't to be that easy, as for days, I was in the doghouse and there was an air of silence when I returned home from work in the evening. I even had to make my own cup of tea in the morning! I had been sent to Coventry by the wife and kids.

As I sat gloomily in the armchair looking out of the window, thinking 'my God, I didn't think it would be as bad as this', I noticed an aeroplane in the sky and began to think 'I wonder?'. The next day I made enquiries, was there a flight to Heathrow to the North East early on a Sunday morning? Yes, there was at 7.30am arriving Teesside an hour later. An elaborate scheme needed to be hatched, this was the plan: we would drive down to the wife's mother in Gloucestershire on the Friday evening.

On the Saturday morning, a work colleague and his wife living in the South West and attending the theatre evening, would pick us up and take us to London, the wife returning with them the following day. Early Sunday morning, I would catch a taxi to Heathrow and fly to Teesside where a friend would be waiting to collect me and take me to the A19 Crathorne junction. I arranged for the Moordale coach travelling to Sheffield to pick me up en route at 9.30am. Everything went like clockwork, the kids and their grandmother eagerly greeted each other, the wife thoroughly enjoyed the theatre and all the trimmings. She even kissed me goodbye early on the Sunday morning wishing the lads good luck.

The taxi driver taking me to Heathrow turned out to be a Chelsea supporter; not many words were exchanged and I can't remember tipping him either. At the departure lounge, I telephoned my friends back that things were running to plan.

The arrival at Teesside was right on time and with no luggage to collect, I was out of the terminal and on my way to Crathorne intersection within minutes. The coach arrived on schedule, I was on the last leg. Arriving at Hillsborough was indeed an achievement in itself.

As often before, Sunderland were the underdogs to the occasion. Their dismal performances earlier in the season had led to the dismissal of Denis Smith. Malcolm Crosby, acting manager, had won over the vast majority of Roker fans, who were pressuring Bob Murray and the board to appoint him as manager. We were on a wave of euphoria, even Bob Murray was laughing and smiling. John Byrne had scored in every match leading up to the semi-final and it was befitting that he should be on the end of a perfect Atkinson cross to deliver the only goal.

It was a truly magnificent afternoon. The atmosphere was perfect and the behaviour of both sets of fans exemplary. There was the exchanging of hats and scarves after the match. My travels of the day, however, were far from being complete – I had to get back to Gloucestershire. I decided to walk to Sheffield station, some 2 or 3 miles from Hillsborough such was the congestion. I saw little point in catching a taxi or bus.

It was almost as if I was walking on air. Arriving at the station I had an hour or so to kill. The whole platform was alive with Canary supporters, several turned to me to wish Sunderland good luck in the final.

I arrived at Gloucester shortly before 10pm where my wife's step father was waiting to drive the last 12 miles of the day to Stroud. The following morning I returned home with the family. Pulling into the drive and turning off the car engine, I took a deep breath, turned to my family and sighed 'Oh well, All's well that ends well.'

(This memory first appeared in the *Sunderland Echo*)

Sun. April 5th 1992   Att. 40,102   Hillsborough   FA Cup Semi-Final
Sunderland 1 v 0 Norwich City
(Byrne)
Norman, Kay, Rogan, Ball, Hardyman, Rush, Bracewell,
Davenport, Armstrong, Byrne, Atkinson. Sub: Bennett.

Memories of Marco

Jim and Hannah Watson, Chesterfield

Having moved to the East Midlands in the early 80s and with the financial rigours of raising a young family on a teacher's pittance, chances to watch the Lads were limited. Playing in a local league I had suffered endless ribbing about the state of SAFC, including the descent into the 3rd Division, witnessed with great amusement by the entire team on a football tour to Weston-Super-Mare.

However, as fortunes turned in the 87-88 season, the name Marco Gabbiadini began to figure more frequently.

My first sighting of the player who was to become a firm favourite of my family was at Mansfield in April 1988. His physique, bustling style and blistering pace (all desperately–needed) made an instant impact.

As my Sunderland-born daughter, Hannah, approached secondary school age, so her interest in SAFC grew.

Despite maternal misgivings, on Saturday 24th November 1990 Hannah watched Sunderland play for the first time, against Sheffield United at Bramall Lane. She was bowled over by the size and volume of the Sunderland following. On the pitch she was similarly smitten by Marco! She remains coy as to whether it was the girth of his calf muscles or his goal scoring prowess (2 quality goals on the day!) that captivated her but her first bout of footballing hero-worship quickly developed. He was an attractive figure - blond, speedy and aggressive on the pitch - but still someone prepared to answer a young girl's fanmail!

Hannah's deep, increasingly expensive and continued love of SAFC started that day, due in no small measure to Marco. He was a genuinely exciting player at a critical time for the club and for my daughter's interest in football.

Sat. Nov 24th 1990   Att. 19,179   Bramall Lane   Division 1
Sheffield United 0 v 2 Sunderland
(Gabbiadini 2)
Norman, Kay, Hardyman, Bennett, Ball, Owers, Bracewell, Armstrong, Davenport, Gabbiadini, Pascoe.

A Trip to Remember   Kevin Clare, Consett

Consett supporters left early for a 5th Round FA Cup trip to Stoke City . The Mags were also playing away that day at Bolton Wanderers. Funnily enough we had recently been to Bolton in the December to watch the Lads play

In those good old days when it was perfectly within the law to stack the bus up with crates of beer it was hardly surprising not to notice that we had veered off the M62 and were heading for a quick and unexpected visit to Burnden Park. We all thought the driver was joking when he stopped right next to all the Mags buses and then informed us that he was not hanging around after the game and if we were not back on the bus by five he would be away. It was only when the organiser had him by the throat saying if he didn't get the bus out of here he wouldn't have one to drive back, that he changed his mind.

By this stage we had around a thousand Mags stopping in their tracks as they passed this solitary bus draped in red and white scarves .It didn't help our cause to have a big union jack in the back window with "We hate the Mags" emblazoned across the centre.

The driver then produced his charter for the day which was given to him early in the morning and yes it did clearly state that he had to take a bus from the depot to Bolton !!!!. We did question his wisdom as to why it hadn't dawned on him that we were all wearing red and white and that we had been singing anti-Mags songs always the way down. He then dutifully informed us that he had been contracted in from Barnsley (such was the shortage of drivers to accommodate all the Sunderland and Mags fans that were travelling to the cup ties) and that he didn't have a clue about football, as rugby was his sport.

He then proceeded to get off the bus so he could ring the depot (long before the days of mobiles). This wouldn't have been a problem but he left the door open as he wandered off in search of a phone.

By this time there were a group of about 30 Mags trying to push the bus over and it was swaying merrily side to side. I have never seen so many drunken fans sober up so quickly .We did manage to stop the Mags getting on the bus by forming a large group at the entrance and then booting any one who tried to get up the steps.

The driver did return and we set back on our way saluting the many thousands of Mags who were walking to the ground in a way you would expect Sunderland fans to greet Mags!!!

I swear by the Almighty that after half an hour along the M62 west bound we saw a bus load of Mags travelling eastbound. And yes you have guessed it, they were on a bus from the same company as we were using, no doubt on their way back from Stoke.

All this for a game, which ended up 0-0

(But we won the replay 2-1. Ed)

Sat. Feb 14th 1976   Att. 41,176   Victoria Ground   FA Cup Rnd 5
Stoke City 0 v 0 Sunderland
Montgomery, Malone, Bolton, Towers, Clarke, Moncur, Kerr, Ashurst,
Holden, Robson, Finney.

Have you Ever been to Blackpool?

Billy Vincent, Sunderland

Have you ever been haunted by a particular phase? Most of us have from time to time, haven't we?

During the first three weeks of my National Service, in the bed right opposite mine, in our barrack room, slept a little, fat guy who hailed from the famous holiday resort of Blackpool. Most of us are proud of our birthplace but this lad was a complete chauvinist. Everyone who came within ten paces of him was targeted with the phrase: "Have you been to Blackpool?" in that Lancashire accent that always reminded me of stand-up comedians.

Our room was forever filled with that plaintive bleat: "Have you ever been to Blackpool?" We scrubbed and blancoed webbing to it; polished shoes and brasses to it and if this Lancastrian could have had his way, no doubt, we would have marched and done arms drill to it. Even today, more than fifty years later, if I have a bad night I seem to hear that voice, trembling somewhere in space: "Have you been to Blackp-o-o-o-l?"

I had great pleasure, before we parted, telling the man from Blackpool: "I have not been to Blackpool, I don't want to go to Blackpool and if I am blessed in future years, I shall never go to Blackpool."

Ironically I did, many years later, travel to the famous seaside resort to enjoy a most satisfying and enlightening football experience; in fact, a total revelation even though we suffered a devastating seven nil drubbing.

We travelled by train, Ronnie and I right across to the other side of the country to the place where Alan Brown, the manager, was expected to introduce his new signing. £18,000 was what he cost, a fabulous fee for a bit kid of eighteen years, who most of us had never heard of. Never mind, we were off to see Blackpool; not to see the illuminations but their star studded football team and perhaps our new boy.

We took our stand near one of the corner flags and had not long to wait before our team ran out in their red and white stripes. I noticed him straight away, the new lad. He was big with well-set shoulders and strong supple legs. I watched the way he moved. He looked good. He looked the part. He was powerful and athletic. The big question was: Did he have what it takes? Eighteen years. He was only a young'n and he was facing a forward line capable of tearing to shreds any defence in the country or anywhere else.

"Come on son, you can do it," I can remember half saying and half praying. We had a poor team at the time and I wondered if this was a suicidal move by Alan Brown. The ref's whistle set the game in motion and Blackpool did what they liked. They were scintillating. In all sections of the pitch they had stars who were already part of football history and, as I have said, we were not a team of all the talents.

I grew tired of seeing our goalie picking the ball out of the back of the net. I was sick. They were walking all over us. My ultra-critical eye locked onto our new player. I examined his play searching for faults. I studied his composure; I checked his every move; his trapping and his passing, his heading and his tackling and could not criticise him. Blackpool

The ideal present for the true SAFC fan! Collage by editor's daughter, Christmas present from the 90s

FOOTBALL MAGAZINE

SUNDERLAND

JOHN HAWLEY

BACK ROW: (L to R) Kevin ARNOTT, Tim GILBERT, Jack ASHURST, Joe BOTTON, Gordon CHISHOLM, Wayne ENTWISTLE (now Leeds), Shaun ELLIOTT.

CENTRE ROW: (L to R) Charlie FERGUSON (chief scout), Joe BOTTON, Steve WHITWORTH, Mike HENDERSON, Ian WATSON, Barry SIDDALL, Chris TURNER, Alan BROWN, Jeff CLARKE, John WATTERS (physio).

FRONT ROW: (L to R) George HERD (youth coach), Mick BUCKLEY, Will ROSTRON, Frank CLARK (asst.manager), Ken KNIGHTON (manager), Gary ROWELL, Bryan ROBSON, Peter EUSTACE (reserves manager).

Sunderland promotion team 1979-80 Joe "Botton" – what a good player he was!

The Reign of Peter Reid

Highs

Staying up 1995
Champs Div. 1 1996
Championship winners 1999
(Record105 points)
Prem. 7th place 2000
Prem. 7th place 2001

Lows

Prem. relegation 1997
Play-off defeat 1998
Prem. cracks appear 2002
Nightmare relegation 2003

Reid on 2003 Relegation in 'The Guardian' Sat 24th Sept 2005, "Probably my biggest problem was the refusal of top players to sign for Sunderland."

"Lilian Laslandes looked the part when I watched him play for Bordeaux against top teams but turned out to be a total disaster for Sunderland. I couldn't believe a player who had looked so good could be so bad for us."

"West Ham came in for Don Hutchison who had been an important player for me and he left us to join them which then caused other of my better players such as Kevin Philips, Gavin McCann, Tommy Sorensen and Michael Gray to start wondering about their futures."

"Some players simply struggled to live up to the raised expectations (of two 7th finishes)."

Supermick

(C. Gambles)

Michael Bridges seen outside Roker in 1996. What a talent – man of the match on his debut v Port Vale, despite only playing the last 20 minutes. Had some memorable performances but was never able to break the Quinn/Phillips partnership. A big money transfer to Leeds followed where he top-scored before injuries effectively ended his top-flight career. On his return to Sunderland in 2004 he was unable to recapture his old form.

(G.Davies)

Superbus

The Wingate Bus, part of Sunderland folklore.

Wingate branch attempt to hide their bus from prying eyes, before clambering aboard for the journey to the match.

Sunderland maul the Magpies

The second of our two famous 'we always win 2-1' successes. Sorensen's penalty save from Shearer will live long in the memory.

(R.Pearce)

The 'scribble' on the ticket is in fact the autographs of Don Hutchison, Niall Quinn, Tommy Sorensen and Peter Reid. Alan Shearer tried to sign but missed.

Passion!

(Pictures: Lee Smith)

Joe Bolton
SAFC 315 app
12 g

Barry Siddall
SAFC 189 app

Charlie Hurley
SAFC 400 app
26 g

SAFC 'characters'

Kevin Ball
SAFC 375 app
27 g

John Kay
SAFC 236 app
0 g

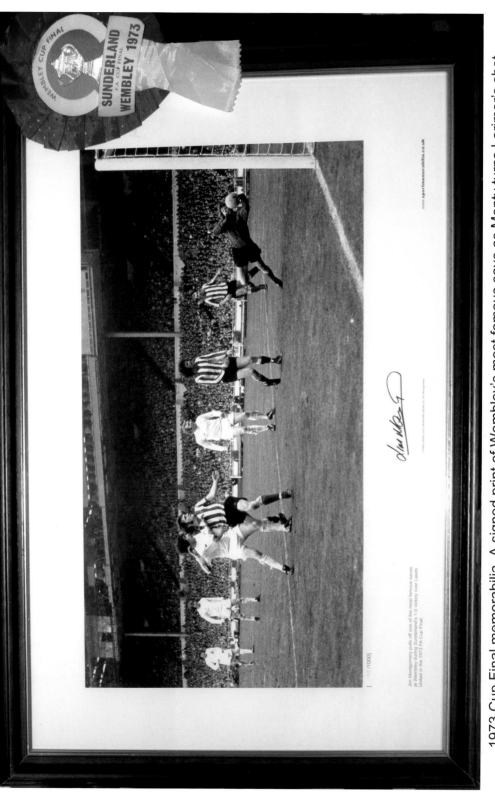

1973 Cup Final memorabilia. A signed print of Wembley's most famous save as Monty turns Lorimer's shot against the bar. The original rosette was worn with pride on that most wonderful of days.

Walk on…walk on

(Ray Hitchison)

Walkers at rest. Nick Pickering (left), Bobby Kerr (centre) and Eric Gates take a breather on the Billingham SAFCSA Branch annual charity walk.
It's good to see ex-players still involved with the Club and supporters' branches, especially on such a worthy charitable effort as this.

A happy band of walkers at journey's end. Billingham Branch charity walk, 2005.

1972/73 Sunderland squad.

A fine but futile win

Anderson (447 app, 35 g)

Kichenbrand (54 app, 28 g)

Stan Anderson (left) and Don Kichenbrand (below) who both played in the 2-0 victory at Portsmouth in 1958. Despite Kichenbrand's 2 goals Sunderland's 68 year unbroken membership of the top division finally ended.

(Topical Times)

Anderson played for all three Northeast teams in an illustrious career, whereas 'Rhino' (on account of his large nose) arrived from Rangers and made only 54 apps before returning to his native South Africa in 1960.

(100 years of Scottish Football)

1956/7

1969/70

1967/8

1994/5

1988/9

1985/6

1975/6

1987/8

1991/2

1978/9

1998/9

1990/91

1982/3

1997/8

2004/5

1996/7

1974/5

2000/1

1992/3

1983/4

50 Years of programmes.

"Film star good looks, blond hair, skill to die for" and scored in every round up to the 1992 Cup Final.

43 app, 15 g (7 in 1992 Cup run)

A newspaper cutting of John Byrne's winning goal in the 1991/2 FA Cup Semi-Final against Norwich 'on the day Bob laughed'. What a pity they both were unable to repeat their feats in the 2-0 Final defeat to Liverpool, bah, bah, bah!

Keep the Faith

Post-match reactions

(Lee Smith)

The Fulwell End at Roker Park in all its splendour

Memories are made of this

(A.King/G.Biggs)

seemed to overrun us every time they got the ball and were piling up the goals, yet, I could find no fault with this bairn who had stepped in the boots of George Aitken.

George Aitken, by the way, was standing almost within touching distance of us; his hands in the pockets of his buff-coloured, double-breasted Mackintosh; a hard man with a world of footballing experience. I tried to guess what was going on in his mind. I still try to guess what was going on in his mind. Was he pleased with the result of Alan Brown dropping him or was he forlorn at the sight of his side being devastated?

Our new centre half was like a red and white striped beacon of hope amidst a thunderous sea of tangerine waves that were battering at every angle, roaring ever onwards, with a glut of goals that threatened to beat all records. The play was hectic, Blackpool were sizzling and in the middle of this turmoil was this boy, calm, cool and collected. I watched him run to the ball, lift his left foot over it and give it a hitch kick with his right, into the path of one of his team mates. His composure was unbelievable. I had seen great centre halves: Frankie Brennan, Neil Franklin, Billy Wright and I felt that this boy would end up in their class. As it turned out, as the years rolled by, Charlie Hurley proved to be a greater centre half than any of them.

We left the corrugated iron stadium that day carrying a 7-0 hammering on our backs, Charlie himself having scored one of those agonising goals, not hearing the distant strains of The Dead March and unable to lift our chins off the pavement, but with the knowledge that we now had at our club a star around whom we could build success. Relegation? Yes, we lost our First Division status that year, despite having a peerless master at the centre of our defence. One man, no matter how good, does not make a team.

"Aye, I have been to Blackpool," I would tell that Lancastrian, if I ever met him again. "And I'm very glad I went, for it was there that I witnessed the tortuous birth of a truly great footballer. A star who will forever sparkle in the Sunderland firmament.

Sat. Oct 5th 1957   Att. 33,172   Bloomfield Road   Division 1
Blackpool 7 v 0 Sunderland
Fraser, Hedley, McDonald, Anderson, Hurley, Elliott, Hannigan, Revie, Spence, O'Neill, Grainger.

A Hitch Unkind Saves Time   Tony Barker, Middlesbrough

We were driving to an away match at Burnley sometime in the 70s when it happened and I'm still not sorry.

Many of the lads preferred just to power on down the A19, A1, then hit the motorways but we were happier trundling across country on the quieter roads and so it was we turned right past Harrogate and along the A59 towards Skipton. All of this might have been lovely in June but it was winter, murky and a tad on the foggy side.

Still, we were in good spirits as we crossed the moors and to be honest being in a car with your mates when the elements are doing their best to spoil your day adds to the whole enjoyment. We'd passed probably the most godforsaken bit when our attention was drawn to a lone figure forlornly trying to hitch a lift. What immediately tugged at the heartstrings was the red and white woollen scarf he was wearing, a soulmate no doubt on his way to Turf Moor.

Never let it be said that Sunderland supporters don't stick together. We began to slow down to offer him a lift, when suddenly the most eagle-eyed among us spotted the letter M, then an A, on the white parts of his scarf.

'It's a Man U fan!' came the cry. He was no doubt on his way to Old Trafford from John O'Groats or somewhere.

With acceleration the envy of a Grand Prix driver we roared past spewing a rain of roadside grit behind us and leaving the bedraggled, and by now apoplectic, Man United fan to his fate.

Well, we couldn't make ourselves late to see the Lads could we?

Oh we do like to be beside the seaside

Freddie Rowe, Horden

One season in the early seventies the fixture computer came up with consecutive away games on the Saturday and Monday of August Bank Holiday; Brighton and Blackpool. We couldn't miss an opportunity for a seaside special, so five of us took advantage of an offer from a local car hire firm. Cheap weekend rates and no mileage excess.

We set off in a brand new Ford Consul on the Friday morning and stayed overnight in a plush London hotel (one of those over the road from Kings Cross Station). We drove to Brighton on the Saturday, went to the match (a battling 2-2 draw) and stayed in a B&B in Brighton, all five of us in one room.

On the Sunday we drove up to Blackpool, stopping several times as the Consul was overheating. Can't imagine why, but it was surely nothing to do with high speed. After an overnight stay in Blackpool, and the match on the Monday (a glorious 0-0) we drove home, knackered but happy with an unbeaten tour and returned the car to the hire company.

Sometime later we had another south coast trip and decided to hire the same car once more.

'No, I'm not hiring it out again,' said the car hire bloke. 'We have had cars returned after a weekend with a thousand miles put on the clock.' We thought it wise not to mention the overheating.

Faith Restored

Roy Logan, Belfast

My world almost came to an end on the 6 May 1972.

It was Cup Final day and the unstoppable Leeds United had just beaten Arsenal by the only goal of the game.

I was a final year student at Trinity College, Dublin University and with just three weeks to my own "finals" had taken the day off to watch the match in "The Silver Tassie" pub, named after the famous Sean O'Casey play.

Leaving the pub after the final whistle the car I was travelling in punctured a front tyre and crashed into a telegraph pole, colliding with the door I was sitting at in the back seat. The three others in the car were unhurt apart from a couple of grazes but I got enough injuries for them all!

Paralysed from the chest down and with massive internal injuries, things looked bleak. My heart stopped in the ambulance that had picked me up and I was quickly resuscitated. A five hour series of operations in the Meath Hospital patched me up inside – spleen removed, diaphragm sewn together again, kidney repaired, stomach reattached, punctured lung fixed up – and my family were called and told to start praying.

Eight months later after another operation and long weeks of rehabilitation I was walking again, albeit with a limp that I still carry today. And today I am one of the last surviving passengers in that car; the driver sadly passed away after a battle with cancer and one other passenger was knocked down and killed in the mid-eighties; the fourth I lost touch with.

And so to SAFC and the point of all this. I was born and still live in N Ireland and started supporting Sunderland in the mid-1960s mainly because I liked the 'candy stripes' but also because a couple of famous N. Ireland players were with them – Johnny Crossan and Martin Harvey.

Having cheated death the year before, imagine my excitement and pride in May 1973 to see the Famous Cup lifted by wee Bobby Kerr and the men from Roker Park.

That it happened almost a year to the day (5th May) since my car accident was the best anniversary present I could ask for; fate and the hand of God had saved me a year earlier and this was part of my reward.

For another almost 30 years I followed Sunderland from a distance – it was always the first result I wanted to know; but family and work meant I couldn't see them as often as I would have liked.

Then in 2000 my wife Vicki spied a small article-cum-advert in the local N Ireland sports paper "The Saturday Night." It was from a Sunderland fan wanting to set up a branch here in N Ireland. I got in touch and the rest, as they say, is history.

I am the Liaison officer for the Branch and still keep the faith and watch the lads at every opportunity. Every season is a roller coaster ride as a Sunderland supporter and you never know whether you will come off the rails or make it to the station! But one thing is for sure, it's never boring and it's never predictable. And having been there myself I can concur with Bill Shankly – football is not a matter of life or death – it's much more important than that.

Random Recollections   Editor

Every so often something unexpected happens which creases you up. I share three such moments;

Away at Rotherham 1988, won 4-1. Superman, not the real one, but dressed for the job and *much* the worse for wear, being carried out of the ground on a stretcher by two doddery old St John Ambulance men. Classic. Who needs kryptonite?

Away at Barnsley 1995, lost 2-0. Mate being questioned by police about his comb being an offensive weapon and a passer by remarking, "Aye you could give someone a nasty quiff with that!"

Away at Everton 2003, lost 2-1. Bloke absolutely fast asleep (again much the worse for wear), head resting on the back of the bloke in the seat in front, then being totally shocked and bewildered by the pandemonium following a Kilbane goal. No idea where he was. Wish I'd have had a video.

Quiz 3

Monty's cryptic Player Quiz

The answers are all Sunderland players. In brackets is the number of appearances they made, followed by the year they left the club.

(Answers on p 128)

1   Opposite to lenders (307) 1994

2   Didn't stay long enough to meet Delilah (14) 1994

3   Minor wedding assistant for this winger (71) 1965

4   Heavenly figure? Hellish for us! (11) 1996

5   Very ordinary early transfer deal (43) 1905

6   Was Harry in the gangster's mob? (33) 1967

7   Defender at home in the Lion's den (45) 1986

8   Sour soul in midfield (106) 1990

9   Cinderella had a good time there (369) 1999

10   Out on his own – not a demon barber (188) 1971

11   Collier or commentator (54) 1973

12   Sounds braver than any other keeper (29) 1986

Welsh Rare Bits

John McKay, York (ex-Houghton)

We'd been drawn away at Cardiff in the FA Cup Round 4 in 1972 so we decided to leave Houghton at midnight on Friday following a 'busy' night out, and wearily arrived in Cardiff just before nine. We quickly discovered the bad news from people in a car behind us who were waving at us and mouthing that the game was off.

We could barely believe it and pulled into a large car park so we could decide what to do. There was some lightening of the mood as our driver from West Rainton chirpily asked the car park attendant, "Does tha tak English money?"

We later discovered through talking to the locals that Cardiff City had announced on the radio that the game was off owing to snow. We found this very hard to believe as the very light snow which had already fallen had melted so we decided to go along to Ninian Park to see for ourselves. We gained access through a small side gate and true there was a light dusting of snow on the pitch, but green could be seen nearly all over and a postponement seemed ridiculous.

Fortunately the pubs were open all day as Wales were playing Scotland in the Five Nations Rugby Championship so we decided to drink away our day before a 5 o'clock journey home. The landlord of the pub was convinced that the rugby international was the real reason the game was off and we were inclined to agree with him. We met some rather unpleasant locals in the form of two skinheads – remember them? – who taunted us, "Tell us where your bus is and we'll see you later."

John Burnhope of Brandon Colliery sprang to his feet, stared them in the eye and stated, "Tell you what, we'll see you now." They made a hasty and undignified exit.

On the long journey back we'd agreed to stop at Worcester for evening refreshments following our day without football. By this time I was worse for wear and as the lads all clambered out in search of a pint I said I'd find them later if I felt like it. Within minutes however a wildly excited Dave Wheatley came banging on the bus window yelling, "Ha'way John, come on Hereford have held the Craas." (Houghton-speak for Mags, Ed)

I was up like a shot, totally rejuvenated and joined our ecstatic group as we went in search of a tv to watch *Match of the Day* to round off not such a bad trip after all.

Some eight years later we were back in the Welsh capital as the end of a promotion season came in sight. Again we travelled on a Friday night passing a huge amount of Sunderland traffic heading to Wales including an old ambulance seemingly held together by string and tape with a sign hanging off the back reading 'Cardiff or bust'. I wonder if it ever got there?

By noon the locals could barely believe the thousands of Mackems milling around the castle area and adjoining streets. We were approached by a policeman who suggested, "There's about 10,000 coming down isn't there boys?"

We replied that it was more like 15,000. "I (Welsh expletive) knew it. Come and tell the Inspector." We agreed and on repeating our info he checked further and discovered the M4 and motorways to the North were chock full of SAFC coaches.

Kick off was delayed at least three times owing to the numbers and Sunderland fans packed three sides of the ground with the Cardiff supporters being huddled in the centre stand. We clinched an important draw and on the Sunday the Welsh TV soccer programme praised the Sunderland travelling support for their huge turn out and impeccable behaviour. As usual.

Sat. May 3rd 1980   Att. 19,340   Ninian Park   Division 2

Cardiff City 1 v 1 Sunderland

(Robson)

Turner, Whitworth, Hinnigan, Clarke, Hindmarsh, Elliott, Arnott, Buckley, Brown, Robson, Cummins. Sub used: Dunn.

Back of the net   Joe Boyle, Cardiff

There comes a point for some of us – the arrival of children, working at weekends, living in South Wales, that sort of thing – when going to the match becomes near impossible. A trip to the SOL is a once-a-year pilgrimage and you pray that any local fixtures don't coincide with the playgroup's Christmas fete or the mother-in-law's birthday ("Why don't you go with just the kids? She can't stand me anyway." "Because you're the only one that drives..." "But what about the match? It's my only chance to see the lads all season." "Don't be so selfish; there's always next year.")

In the days when I was a regular attender, the football was almost incidental to my enjoyment of match day. Of course, I always wanted a win and a bad result could ruin the weekend. But what was more important was the shape of the day, the predictable routines, the people you spent the day with. Home games would start with Football Focus. Then a short drive, parking in the same spot, a couple of pints at the Harbour View, a quick rendezvous outside the club shop, the same spot on the Fulwell End, the match, Final Score back at the Harbour View and Sports Report on the drive home.

Away games would have their routines too: Danny Baker on the outward journey (when he still did his pre-match show), a pit-stop at the

Wetherby Whaler, 606 on the way back.

At the heart of it all was the banter, the friends you'd make, the characters you'd meet. I didn't care what division we were in, whether there was a packed weekend house or 12,000 of us shivering midweek, whether it was Liverpool or Luton.

As I say, those days have gone but I still hanker after the shared experience that going to the game offered and in the last couple of years have discovered a very satisfactory substitute: the internet.

For Sunderland fans, the key online destination has to be a site called Readytogo.net. Although it provides news (generally second-hand), the main focus is the message board. Almost 3,000 people have registered to use it, some who are regulars, some who look in once and are never seen again. Alter-egos are carefully constructed and, although some people become personal friends and meet up at well-attended social events, half the fun is the anonymity, wondering just who it is that goes by the name 'Partridge amongst the pig' (according to his profile, he comes from South Shields and lists his occupation as 'moron'. Ring any bells?)

But for someone miles distant from Wearside, the forum offers a superb insight into the atmosphere surrounding the club. In terms of a pure debate about the state of the club, the key figure is "My Boy Harry", virulent in his dislike of the current board and convinced that the club will go nowhere until a new regime is in place. He has his backers, he has his opponents, many of whom are put off by his occasionally pompous tone. But the debates about the club that he provokes are, by and large, passionate and intelligently expressed. It's little wonder that figures at the club (including some players, we're led to believe) and local journalists turn to the board to gain a sense of the supporters' mood.

As for match day, I look forward to the regular post-match posting from 'Wheatley Hill East Durham', with his analysis and marks-out-of-ten for each player, which tend to be met by responses such as: 'Brown 5? Eh? Did you have a bag on your head or something? He ran his socks off today and created the first goal from nothing by not giving up a lost cause. Add at least 3.' Then there was Lord Cheese (yes, really) who used to post TV clips of the goals within minutes of the final whistle, until the authorities cottoned on and threatened legal action.

In between matches there's plenty of transfer gossip to chew over. Most famously on this front was the non-transfer of Jan Koller this summer, a false story concocted by six members of the board that was taken up by the press and reported internationally as a done deal until the player was forced to issue a personal denial.

But the football probably counts for less than half of what is discussed on the board. There are regular political run-ins, crudely split between those with liberal leanings (dubbed the 'Sandalistas') and more conservative types, as well as discussions about culture, beer and sex. People come on to announce marriages, births and deaths, in turn receiving heart-felt congratulations and commiserations.

All life is here. In summer 2005 as I write, the top ten topics are:

- 'There's an alien near my office': something to do with a Fathers for Justice protest.
- 'Poster from Notting Hill tube station yesterday': a photo of a handwritten warning that reads, 'Please do not run on the platforms or concourses. Especially if you are carrying a rucksack, wearing a big coat or look a bit foreign.'
- 'Golf phrases': a rather unfunny collection of golfing double entendres.

- 'Will we stop up next season, yes or no': a majority think not.

- 'Woodgate crocked again': includes disbelief that Newcastle could have got such a high fee for the permanently injured defender.

- 'Your opinion of other posters': a discussion on the character and opinions of other users of the message board. Such navel-gazing is a regular feature of the board.

- 'Mick wants three more signings': speculation on who might be inbound.

- 'Michael Shields jailed in Bulgaria': general outrage.

- 'Vauxies Boys reunion (ad Friday's Echo)': details of a boys' day out at The Ashbrooke with Bertie, Slosher and Gunner in attendance.

- 'War on Terror goes national': reaction to the latest arrests in Birmingham following the attacks on London.

In many ways, it's a series of topics that you might discuss in the car on a long away trip. And that's the point. The match day experience may be a thing of the past for me. But in Readytogo.net I've found the next best thing.

Stelling's Surprise

Sandy Phillips, Beaconsfield

Although I live in Beaconsfield, Bucks I am descended from the Phillips family which were part of the famous Wearside pottery Dixon Phillips & Co in the 19th Century. My father gained a job that took him around the country leaving Sunderland in 1937. I was born in Cardiff in 1944 and at the age of 8 begged my father to take me to a game at Ninian Park.

It was in December 1952 and Cardiff had recently been promoted to the first division (equivalent of today's Premiership) and at the time of the match Sunderland were lying top. I am now 61 and maybe this was the last time we were top of the pyramid. There was a large crowd and we were forced to stand very near the front alongside the corner flag.

At the time I think rationing was in place and it was certainly a time when 'travelling supporter' was not a well-known term. Cardiff had a tricky Stanley Matthews-type left winger called George Edwards who would teeter towards his opposing full back and then suddenly dip a shoulder one way and pass the full back on the other side.

By late in the game, being 3-1 down, Sunderland were obviously going to lose and Edwards for the umpteenth time slowly made his way up the wing. I seem to recall Sunderland's right back was Jack Stelling and backed off and backed off, wary of darting in and being left flatfooted by Edwards. My father was infuriated by Stelling backing off and shouted to the latter who was no more than 5 yards away, "Whose side are you on Stelling?"

Poor Stelling, surprised to hear an away supporter 300 miles away from Roker Park, looked up to see where this Sunderland voice was coming from and Edwards flashed inside unopposed and crossed to the centre forward who headed in the 4th goal. At the end of the season Sunderland finished in 9th place but if they had lost the First Division on goal average my father might have had to bear a heavy burden.

Sat. Dec 13th 1952   Division 1   Ninian Park   Division 1
Cardiff City 4 v 1 Sunderland
                    (Ford)
Threadgold, Hedley, Hudgell, Aitken, Hall, A Wright, T Wright,
Watson, Ford, Shackleton, Reynolds.

Howzat?

Brian McCullough, Paddock Wood

As well as supporting SAFC since the early sixties, both my wife and myself follow Kent County Cricket Club around the country during the summer.

I had been to see the lads at Gillingham and QPR and we had both gone up to the Stadium of Light for the match against Coventry. However, due to the overlap in the football and cricket seasons, we were staying in Bristol for Kent's match against Gloucestershire at the time of the match at West Ham. Unfortunately the place we were staying in had no SKY television, but I knew the pub across the road had SKY.

I listened to the first half on the radio in our room, and when we were one down at half time I decided to stay there unless there was a change for the better. When we equalised I decided I could not risk not seeing us win the Championship if we went on to win the game. So I dashed across to the pub only to find that they had the Rugby League on SKY TV! I went further along to the next pub, but they did not even have their TV on.

I was resigned to going back to our room and the radio commentary when I noticed the Coral Bookmakers still had their lights on. I dashed across the road, looked through the window and saw that they had the match on and the score was still 1-1.

Although the racing had long since finished, I tried the door. It was of course locked but the employee inside heard me and came to the door. I explained my dilemma and he invited me in. It turned out he wanted the Lads to win as well – he had a bet running on all four English divisions – Chelsea, SAFC, Luton and Yeovil. When the winner went in there were resounding cheers all around the shop – from the two of us.

The only downside was that my son is a season ticket holder at West Ham (poor upbringing I know!) and I was hoping that they too would at least make the play-offs, but Friday 29th April will live long in my memory – a happy day indeed.

Eventually the story had a happy ending for all concerned – my friend in Bristol won his bet when all four of his teams were successful and West Ham gained promotion via the Play-Offs.

The Houghton Display Team

Stephen Brown, Hetton-le-Hole

The Bristol Rovers v Sunderland game in April 1980 was the most memorable to me because of being away from home for so long and for the scariest visit to the toilet I've ever had in my life.

The game came near the end of our ultimately successful promotion campaign which was completed when we beat the season's FA Cup Winners

West Ham at Roker Park. Our penultimate away match, however, was also just about our longest trip of the season resulting in us having to leave Houghton at midnight on Friday. Prior to this at about six in the evening I had what would turn out to be my last wash and brush up for 32 hours before I and a couple of my mates went through to enemy territory 'The Hofbrauhaus' in New****le and after a bawdy night arrived back in Houghton for departure at nearly midnight, somewhat worse for wear.

After a long journey we reached Bristol at the unearthly hour of seven in the morning meaning there would be a long wait before the pubs opened at eleven. The bus more or less emptied on arrival and supporters went wandering off looking for any cafes serving breakfast whilst others dozed or played football in the car park adjacent to Eastville, Bristol Rovers' ground. I however spent my time reading some 'adult literature' which had conveniently been left on the empty back seat.

The morning dragged but by 10.30 the lads were gathering outside the nearest pub. The thirty minutes before opening seemed like an eternity yet eventually at 11 the sound of locks being opened and bolts drawn back could clearly be heard and the landlady opened the door as she'd done probably thousands of times before when no-one was waiting to come in. This time though she was confronted by the horrifying sight of sixty, scruffy, unshaven Sunderland supporters desperate for entry. She hastily slammed the door before opening it again, composing herself and peeking out. Finally she let us all in with a strict warning not to cause any bother, which of course we didn't, and a pleasant few hours passed drinking and lying in the sunny beer garden.

An hour before kick off we moved into a rather decrepit stadium and massed on the open terrace where we sang our hearts out for the next three hours or so. The match itself was fairly unmemorable, notable only for a rare goal from Barry Dunn, but a 2-2 draw was satisfactory as we were now handily placed for promotion and this made our long journey home more acceptable.

At Birmingham we decided to go up the M6 and then across the Pennines at Tebay and Kirby Stephen across to Scotch Corner. Making good progress we reached Lancaster mid-evening and stopped for a couple of hours drinking. By the time we all drifted back to the coach at closing time we found a most grumpy, restless bus driver who was desperate to be away and we were soon heading northwards on the M6. By now of course our over-filled bladders were screaming for release but the driver refused point blank to pull over saying there'd be no more stops until we reached home. Our pleas grew louder and so unignorable that finally the impasse was overcome (Health and Safety officials please stop reading here.)

The driver opened the door of the bus and pointed outside as we hurtled along at some 60 or 70 m.p.h. A queue then formed down the aisle of the bus with the person at the front standing on the bottom step having a pee out of the door. His only safeguard from oblivion was the next in line holding him from behind. The whole procedure proved successful as long as the bus drove in a straight line, but on bends or over bumps a serious wobble was caused which resulted in the inevitable wet trouser legs. Watching this death-defying pantomime were two women in the front seats who had a brilliant view of all these blokes with their wedding tackle out, and this in the days before male strippers like the Chippendales.

With bladders emptied we 'eventually' reached home and I 'eventually' managed to have a wash, 'eventually' collapsing into bed at 2 o'clock on the Sunday morning, but most importantly, 'eventually' Sunderland won promotion to the top flight at the season's end.

Sat. 19th April 1980   Att. 9,757   Eastville   Division 2

Bristol Rovers 2 v 2 Sunderland

(Robson, Dunn)

Turner, Whitworth, Hinnigan, Clarke, Hindmarsh, Buckley, Arnott, Dunn, Brown, Robson, Cummins.

A Fine but Futile Win   Jerome Hanratty, Tynemouth

Sunderland's most important game ever? Because I was living on the South coast at the time, I was privileged to be present at a fixture where this hackneyed claim had more justification than most. It was the final game of the 1957/58 season – Portsmouth v Sunderland on the 26th April – one which could decide whether the Wearsiders would drop to Division 2 for the first time.

Sunderland had the exclusive record of being the only team never to have played outside the top division; but with only one game left to play they were now second off bottom. Portsmouth were only two points ahead of them but had a better goal average. As rewards then were two points for a win, and relegation was confined to the bottom two clubs, a victory for Sunderland was vital. But it would only keep them up if Leicester City, one point ahead and managed by former Sunderland player Dave Haliday, failed to win a tough away game at Birmingham.

In those pre-motorway days, visiting supporters were rare at distant venues like Fratton Park. It seemed to me I was the only Sunderland supporter in a crowd of 22,500 but that did not stop me cheering them on as the teams ran out and the band played 'The Pompey Chimes'. Then an away supporter could shout for his team in an unsegregated crowd without the risk of being half killed.

The pressure of the occasion was evident as the game began. On a wet and muddy pitch there were nervous mistakes and some frantic running about before the team settled down. Manager Alan Brown had been criticised for his selection of older players – omitting, for example the youthful Billy Bingham – but the maturity of the veterans proved valuable at this stage. The team, in fact did have a share of youth and experience; I remember a thundering shot from Don Revie and then his elegance and generalship dovetailing into the persistence of Anderson and Pearce as Sunderland began to take grip on midfield. Behind them the ageing but uncompromising defence of Hedley and Elliot provided a perfect foil for the skills of the young Hurley, whose head seemed to dominate every Pompey attack.

As the game went on, the classy Grainger on the left wing regularly pulled down crossfield passes, beat his man and put over the fast low centres he was noted for. Waiting for them, the giant Kichenbrand was as ungainly as we ever remembered him: miskicking, missing the goal, and just seeming to flounder. Yet he was in the right spot just before half time when Ambrose Fogarty, the 'human dynamo', pushed the ball through to the centre forward position; Rutter, the Portsmouth centre half slipped in the mud and Kichenbrand hoofed it home from close in.

During a chain-smoking second half growing in tension, a desperation seemed to return to the team as Portsmouth inspired by Jimmy Dickinson, began to mount a succession of attacks. Billy Elliot who was being sorely tried by Portsmouth's right winger Harris kicked out from under the bar and at one point little Alan O'Neill (formerly called Hope – a name he should have retained for this game) threw himself on top of the ball and wouldn't get up. But Fogarty kept on running, Fraser stayed safe in goal and Charlie Hurley was magnificent.

Then came the perfect finale. Stan Anderson won the ball and sent a long pass through to Kichenbrand who hooked it past Uprichard in the Portsmouth goal. That brought Kichenbrand's total to 6 goals in ten appearances – a ratio he maintained and a fact we tend to forget when remembering his shortcomings. A minute after that goal the final whistle from Mr R. J Leafe spelt final relief. We had won!

Standing in the bus queue after the game I snatched at the football edition of the Portsmouth Evening News. It said: Birmingham City 0 Leicester City 1. We were down!

Sunderland had finished with 32 points. That was the same total as Portsmouth and – to rub salt in the wound – the same as Newcastle United. So we went down into the Second Division on goal average along with Sheffield Wednesday. Sunderland had at last lost their record – but it was not until 1988, 30 years on, that another team, Arsenal equalled that total of 68 consecutive seasons in the top league.

Sunderland's progress since that fateful Spring of 1958 has been nothing to shout about, apart from the brief intermission on 1973. Several relegations have come our way, not to mention the delights of the Freight Rover Trophy. Yet for those of us who remember that day those years ago no subsequent indignity has matched what happened then. To paraphrase the words of Dylan Thomas – after the first relegation, there is no other.

(This memory first appeared in *A Love Supreme*)

Sat. April 26th 1958   Att. 22,545   Fratton Park   Division 1
Portsmouth 0 v 2 Sunderland
(Kichenbrand 2)
Fraser, Hedley, Elliott, Anderson, Harley, Pearce, Revie, O'Neill, Fogarty, Kichenbrand, Grainger.

I have not seen as much of the Lads over the years as I should have, or should have liked to. But I am still a devoted fan from way down south, having chosen to support them simply because I liked the sound of the word Sunderland at the age of 8. No one else at school supported that team (most of them were Luton or Watford, the local sides), and I wanted to be different. At that age I thought Sunderland sounded like a sun-kissed Caribbean island. I saw most of the 1973 cup run, including of course the gripping final, and usually catch them once or twice a season. The last game I saw was the 2-2 draw at Ipswich this year. I am now a trustee of the Sunderland AFC Foundation and it's amazing to think how a choice made at eight years of age could have had such an outcome and given me such close involvement with this wonderful club.

'Sunderland Expects that Every Man will do his Duty'

Michael Harrison, Harrogate

I had been to Wembley before to support Sunderland (all losses of course…) but had always travelled down and back on the day. As a result, I had hated these experiences, especially the length of journey, which of course seemed twice as long coming back!

So, when we played Charlton in the 1998 play-off I decided to do what I had always fancied, travel down the night before and have a night out 'on the lash.' That way, even if the result was bad, I would have enjoyed at least part of the experience.

Having travelled down the night before I found myself out in the centre of London with a friend. "We must be in Trafalgar Square for last orders" was the instruction. I didn't care what we did or where we went in the evening but we had to be in Trafalgar Square for lasts. I didn't really know why I had to be there: I'd been told it was a laugh; I'd been told it was traditional, but nothing quite prepared me for the sight at about 10.30pm.

There were Sunderland supporters just everywhere, cheering, singing and swimming (in the fountain). Perched on top of the base of Nelson's Column seemed the place to be, and sure enough I found myself on there, slightly (well, very) drunk, and at 5'5" I ended up with bruises and scrapes on my shins trying to get up there. (You can imagine the conversation with my wife later when she saw the bruises...."How did you get those?"...erm...."climbing up Nelson's Column?!")

Anyway, after what seemed an eternity, where the whole place seemed to be red and white stripes (there were two teams playing the next day weren't there?), my friend and I lowered ourselves from Nelson, and started walking away from the square. As we moved away from the throng, a lady tugged my arm and introduced herself as a tourist from Canada: "So, what exactly have you guys won?" she asked.

"Nothing missus," came the answer. "We don't play until tomorrow."

I'll never forget the look of absolute bewilderment on this woman's face. She must have been thinking, "If you haven't even played yet, why all this singing and throwing yourselves in the fountain?" Of course the answer was that we were Sunderland Supporters. And that is all anyone needs to know.

Mon. May 25th 1998   Att. 77,739   Wembley   Div 1 Play-off Final
Charlton Athletic 4 v 4 Sunderland
[Charlton won 7-6 on penalties]
(Quinn 2, Phillips, Summerbee)
Perez, Holloway, Gray, Craddock, Williams, Clark, Summerbee, Ball,
Quinn, Phillips, Johnston. Subs: Makin, Rae, Dichio.

The Legend That Will Never Die!   Clive Lee, Hetton

Sunderland's famous cup run turned the whole place around, cup fever on Wearside spread like wildfire. We kept saying; is this really happening? Is it true? They reckon you can lose sleep over worry and certainly in my lifetime you can lose sleep through sheer joy. Eventually once you did get to sleep, and you woke there was this wonderful realisation that YES! It really was bloody happening it really wasn't a dream. You really were witnessing history in the making.

Having missed out on the semi-final against Arsenal when our ballot tickets did not come out of the draw, I was sickened and sad not to see our heroes at Hillsborough, having gone to every round with my dad and brothers. But my dad, old faithful himself, had kept hold of our ballot tickets in full belief that Sunderland would go all the way to Wembley, after beating the cockneys. Of course they didn't let us down, beating them 2-1, with two great goals from the H-bombs, Halom and Hughes to go through and play the mighty Leeds United. I can remember dancing around the living room like some crazed believer, having witnessed a miracle occur. After the victory I can remember going out into our back lane and kicking hell out of a ball against the back yard wall, re-creating every move, hammering a beautiful volley and yelling, "IT'S A GOAL! By Halom!" at the top of my voice and, like some possessed soul, loosening a few bricks in the process.

On the Monday after the game, the draw for the tickets was made on Radio Newcastle. I can remember running home from Bede School to listen to it. When our ballot tickets had come out of the draw, it was pure joy. My dad, our Robert and Derek and myself had a ticket each. I was only 14 at the time and my dreams had come true.

The weeks leading up to the final were like waiting for Christmas, I could think nothing but WEMBLEY! I was even off my food, which was a rare thing for me! Cup Fever had badly set in, and all I could think about was the lads running out at Wembley. This might be hard to believe, if I have to drop down dead writing this now, I don't really care, because the Christmas before our cup run had ever happened I can actually remember asking my dad would he take me to Wembley if Sunderland ever reached the final. I can remember him grinning and saying, "Yes son I'll take you if ever the lads get to Wembley!" probably thinking they have as much chance as himself making Prime Minister and moving to number 10 Downing Street! But the footballing gods must have listened and granted my request.

The whole town was gripped by cup fever; even my mother got carried away and got cup fever. She did up the whole front room window with newspaper cuttings like 'STOKOE THE MESSIAH' 'SUNDERLAND IN WONDERLAND' The town had gone stark raving mad, and was painted red and white. Everywhere you went, people were asking for cup tickets, I think my father had ours in the bank! I can remember thinking, "What if someone robs the bloody bank? It would be a disaster!" My brother Robert was walking round delivering his newspapers with headlines from newspapers stapled onto his parka coat like "STOKOE FOR GOD", "KING

WATSON", "WEARSIDE MANIA".

I can remember getting on an old clapped out banger of a bus at Park Lane at midnight on the Friday night; we were to travel all night to London, and I can't remember getting much sleep. The older lads had been round a few pubs and were in good voice with songs like "VIC HALOM-VIC HALOM-VIC HALOM-da da da da da!" and "Now you're going to believe us, we're going to win the cup!" Everyone had red and white boaters on, scarves, banners. Every time the bus went down a hill, rivers of pee swilled down the bus, but who cared? We were the chosen ones to go to Wembley and nothing was going to stop us now, even if it felt like the back wheel had dropped off, the bus was so old! I think I only slept for an hour, but when I did I can remember dreaming I was at Wembley, and Sunderland had been awarded a penalty kick in the dying minutes, and my very own self had to take it, and blasting it into the net past Leeds goalkeeper David Harvey. But at that moment my dad spoilt my goal celebrations, and said, "Do you want the toilet?" as we pulled into a service station.

Arriving in London at about 7am, it was all such a big place to me, having never been there in my life. Our dad took us to all the sights (not Soho), though I did enquire why all the older lads on our bus had kept mentioning it! The whole morning it rained cats and dogs, but I hung about cafes as we were a bit too young for the stronger stuff!

I remember walking down Wembley Way and looking at those Twin Towers, and you know what – the Taj Mahal couldn't have looked better. My dream of walking down Wembley Way had finally arrived and no one was going to take it away from me!

Near the stadium a massive game of footy was going on in the car park, about 60 on each side, between both sets of fans and neither side was taking any prisoners. They were taking lumps out of each other, Doc Martens flying about all over. Sunderland won about 18-0! First blood to Sunderland! I knew it then that it was going to be Sunderland's day.

Once inside the stadium, after desperately clinging onto my ticket as if my life depended on it, I remembered my dad's words, "Hang onto it inside your pocket," but no-one was going to take this passport heaven off me, I would have fought to the death. As I entered the stadium, I said to myself, "Well Clive mate this is no longer a dream any more, you are really here," and thanked the footballing gods for giving me this sacred day, as we made our way down to the front to witness which would turn out to be the greatest day in my life supporting Sunderland.

The stadium itself was a truly marvellous sight when first entering, huge and with a magical feel about the whole place. But the atmosphere created that day by our magnificent supporters will live long in my memory. Our fanatical fans were absolutely deafening, like a massed tribe of warriors going to war, saluting their heroes. The flags, banners, horns, drums, and the sea of red and white made it feel like a cast iron reassurance that no way we could lose this game today with an army of proud fans like these.

Let battle commence. The lads fought and played if their lives depended on it, it was like some type of war. Leeds were not going to have all their own way today. When Richie Pitt flattened Alan Clarke in the first five minutes, they knew we meant business. When Porterfield scored in the 32nd minute, the scene in the Sunderland end was one of absolute madness! My father lost his red and white boater in the mayhem, and some huge bloke picked me up like a bag of sticks and practically broke my ribs with a bear hug. I remember saying to him, "Don't kill me mister I've got to live to at least the full time whistle." But the feeling was one of pure ecstasy, joy and emotion all rolled into one.

When Monty made his miracle save I knew it just meant to be, nothing could stop us now, not even an earthquake! The final dying minutes were sheer agony, my heartbeat thundering like some pot riveter down at the shipyards. A bloke next to me kept asking the time a dozen times in the space of a minute, in the end I nearly gave him my watch. But at last – the final whistle was blown, the scenes were amazing, grown blokes crying like babies. There was a non-stop chorus of "We've won the Cup" ringing all round Wembley for a solid ten minutes. Little old Sunderland had shocked the whole world and won the bloody cup! I felt totally exhausted, but joy and a realisation, I said to myself, "Clive, your dream has come true, the impossible dream has come true." Strangers were hugging each other like long lost brothers. I looked up at Wembley's huge electronic scoreboard which was there for the whole world to see.

LEEDS 0 SUNDERLAND 1, PORTERFIELD 32 MINUTES.

In all of the years I have supported Sunderland, this momentous day has to be the greatest day I have experienced as a supporter. Nothing has yet eclipsed it. Hopefully someday I can experience it again, when my beloved Sunderland can achieve the same type of success.

Sat. May 5th 1973   Att. 100,000   Wembley   FA Cup Final
Sunderland 1 v 0 Leeds United
(Porterfield)
Montgomery, Malone, Watson, Pitt, Guthrie, Horswill, Kerr,
Porterfield, Hughes, Halom, Tueart.

Mags and Smogs quotes from *The Book of Football Quotations* by Phil Shaw.

"Newcastle has been very unlucky with injuries this season. The players keep recovering"

(Len Shackleton)

"I've heard of players selling dummies, but this club keeps buying them"

(Len Shackleton on the Mags)

"People talk about Newcastle as a sleeping giant. They last won a Championship in 1927, the FA Cup in 1955. They already make Rip van Winkle look like a catnapper"

(Hugh McIlvanney on the Mags)

"Tyneside's very own Renaissance man, capable of breaking both leg and wind at the same time"

(Jimmy Greaves on Gazza)

"He's the only player that when he's on T.V. the Daleks hide behind the sofa"

(Nick Hancock on Peter Beardsley)

"My team mates advised me to visit the place first. I went to have a look at Middlesbrough and decided I was better off at Parma"

(Antonio Benarrivo)

"I started the shirt-lifting thing and I'm still best at it"

(Ravanelli, still struggling with English idioms)

"Don't worry about that, lad. Leave it. Just leave it."

This was my grandad speaking. At about 6.45 am on the morning of the fifth of May 1973.

What had happened was, some girls employed by the Sunderland Echo had been handing out cardboard hats at Sunderland train station to people arriving to board the football specials down to London. I had grabbed about ten of them, dropped one which then blew up in the air and back down in an arc on to the track right in front of the stationary train we were about to board.

Of course, I took my grandad's advice and left it. I did have another nine, after all.

My grandad had been to every single home game since World War Two, or some other such time back in the mists of history. And here we were (he'd somehow managed to get tickets for himself, my uncle and me) up for the Cup Final.

On our way down, an old guy on the train made the time pass with tales of Sunderland's last FA Cup Final appearance, at Wembley in 1937. He had been there and he told me about Raich Carter and Bobby Gurney, and about beating Preston 3-1 after being 1-0 down at half time.

I still have my (yellowing) ticket for this match. It cost one pound, a bit less than a Cup Final ticket at the 'new' Wembley will cost.

By this time of his life, my grandad was in the early stages of his suffering from arthritis, meaning from the start of the following season we would have seats in the Clock Stand rather than standing in the Fulwell End every game. He limped up Wembley Way, and this story is relevant because the thing - the one thing – I recall about the actual match itself is Ian

Porterfield's goal, and my grandad next to me jumping up and down, his nascent arthritis forgotten.

Next thing I knew I was in a sticky-floored, smoky pub waiting for the train back to Sunderland.

Then, on Monday, my schoolmates who hadn't been were trying to tell me it was a lot better watching on the telly than having been there. You can't see anything when you're there, can you ?

Of course, since then, I have seen the video – DVD now, probably - and know all about Richie Pitt's tackle, Monty's save, the yellow ball, and the only Cup Final with no offsides (is this last one true, or an urban myth?)

And maybe some day in the future I will be on another football special on the way to the Cup Final and there will be some ten-year-old lad who I can regale with my stories of the Wembley victory of 1973.

2-0 Ha Ha Ha!   Colin Harrison, Knaresborough

That banner slung over the A52 courtesy of the 'working' Nottingham miners said it all. They thought they'd had the last laugh on that Cup Final day in 1992, but as we know in football nothing's ever quite that straight forward.

The day had begun well with high expectations, but by Scotch Corner in the early morning light the first bad omen appeared. My mate Tim with true Ferryhill hospitality had made mountains of sandwiches and had been so solicitous about just what fillings I preferred. Unfortunately butter has the tendency to make me sick which he hadn't realised, so I merely picked at the ham and pease pudding fillings as we continued our journey south.

After a stop at a service station we proudly hung our scarves out of the windows (driver and passenger) and even now it always brings a lump to my throat to see football scarves like battle standards streaming out of car windows. Bad omen again, as the rain began to pour down, we knew the scarves would be wringing wet but what the hell we were proud of our colours.

By South Mimms those old familiar feelings of hope, anticipation and excitement surfaced, but clouded by the darker ones of fear, foreboding and perennial disappointment. The scarves by now were sopping and realising we were going to get wet necks Tim suggested we took them in to allow them to dry a little.

Once again we negotiated the dubious pleasures of Wembley's arcane parking system and decided we wanted to walk up Wembley Way – it was Cup Final day after all. We hadn't reckoned however with an obstreperous police officer who decided peremptorily that we couldn't cross the road onto the bridge to access Wembley Way and despite remonstrations we were denied that very simple pleasure.

We thus ended up walking around what was in 1992 a disgrace of a National Football Stadium – broken concrete, wire mesh, seediness and the general run down aura of a Third World country.

Eventually we were inside 'And it's Sun-der-land, Sun-der-land F.C'.... creating a tremendous atmosphere. Bring on Liverpool.

Then....bloody John Byrne! Film star good looks, blond hair, lived in

Loyalty

(Lee Smith)

The Division 2 Play-off Final 1990. Following an amazing 2-0 second leg semi-final win at Newcastle, Sunderland played poorly in this Final losing 1-0 to Swindon Town. The hero of the game, Tony Norman, runs out onto the Wembley arena for the pre-match warm-up. Thanks to financial irregularities at Swindon, Sunderland were promoted in their stead but lasted only one year before being relegated in 1991.

Lapel
Badges

SUNDERLAND STARS

JOHN McDOUGALL. A Scottish international who joined Sunderland as a centre-half from Airdrie. Was transferred to Leeds United in 1934.

JIMMY CONNOR. One of the most popular Sunderland players ever. His thrilling raids from the left wing are still talked about. Played four times for Scotland.

BOBBY GURNEY. A great hearted player whose goal scoring feats are legend. His one England cap was a poor reward for such a brilliant forward.

SUNDERLAND 1913. The famous "Team of all Talents" that was a big force in English football in the early part of the century. Back row: Milton, Cringan, Thomas, Butler, Gladwin, Low. Front row: Mordue, Buchan, Hall, Holley, Martin. Insets: Cuggy and Richardson.

TREVOR FORD. The big Welshman caused quite a stir when he moved from Aston Villa to Sunderland. Very popular both for his tremendous ability and his bravery.

RAICH CARTER. Must rate as one of the all-time greats of football. Captained the 1937 Sunderland side at Wembley and then won another winner's medal with Derby County. Was manager of Hull City and Leeds United. Won 13 full England caps and 16 war-time caps.

SUNDERLAND 1937. Here is the team that took the Cup to Sunderland. Alex Hastings the skipper was injured and his place was taken by Sandy McNab pictured below. Back row: Mr. J. Cochrane (Manager), Thomson, Hall, Mapson, A. Reid (Trainer), Gorman, Hastings, Clarke. Front row: Duns, Burbanks, Gurney, Gallacher, Carter (Captain), Johnston.

BILLY BINGHAM. Signed from Glentoran, Billy played in over 200 games during his eight year stay at Roker. Played 56 times for Ireland.

STAN ANDERSON. This fine half back stayed 12 years at Sunderland with over 400 games to his name. Then went to Newcastle and Middlesbrough. Won two full caps.

JIMMY COWAN. Few will forget Jimmy's performance in goal for Scotland at Wembley in 1949. He was then a Morton player but was soon Sunderland bound. Won 25 Scottish caps altogether.

IVOR BROADIS. One of Britain's finest inside forwards, Ivor also played for Newcastle. Now a journalist.

SANDY McNAB was called upon to fill in for the injured Alex Hastings in the 1937 Cup Final and played a brilliant game. He was later transferred to West Bromwich Albion.

JIMMY THORPE. One of the tragedies of football. This brilliant goalkeeper, born in Jarrow. He showed great promise. When he died after a match he was found to be suffering from diabetes.

WILLIE WATSON. A stylish Yorkshireman who played for England at soccer and cricket. Made four England appearances.

ARTHUR HUDGELL. Caused quite a stir when signed from Crystal Palace for a large fee just after the war. He was virtually unknown, but soon showed the justification for his price.

LEN SHACKLETON. The brilliant "Shack" was always in the news if not his superb play it was usually for some act of defiance. A great entertainer.

5th May 1973

Bobby Kerr takes
the cup from the
Duchess of Kent and
Sunderland make
the headlines.

ARTHUR
HOPCRAFT
AT WEMBLEY

Dreams do come true . .

Sunderland 1

W-U-N-D-E-R-LAND

For Stokoe's
men a dream
comes true

'WE WANT STOKOE, WE WANT STOKOE'

ALAN
HOBY
reports

F A Cup Final

SUNDERLAND TRIUMPH MAKES FUTURE LOOK SO MUCH BRIGHTER

By DONALD SAUNDERS

Leeds Utd. ...... 0 Sunderland 1

SUNDERLAND'S triumph over Leeds at
Wembley on Saturday not only ended the
First Division's monopoly of the F A Cup but
further discredited the cautious, jargon-ridden
philosophy that has inhibited English soccer for
far too long.

STOKOED! SUNDERLAND SNATCH THE CUP

The crowd builds before a game then it's all eyes on the match

(Photos Lee Smith)

We're there!

(Barry Robson)

Premiership promotion 2005 finally achieved at home to Leicester is confirmed only following an agonising wait for the Ipswich result at Leeds to be announced.

The Championship was clinched away at West Ham and eventually the trophy was paraded with pride on a procession through the city. (below)

(Lee Smith)

2

3

4

5

(1)   SAFCSA badges from the 1960s
(2)   1930s logo
(3)   An inflatable from the 1990s
(4)   Samson and Delilah
(5)   Monty the Black Catalogue cat

(Lee Smith)

Goalmouth action from the final game of the 2004/5 season. Simonsen the Stoke 'keeper repels a Sunderland attack. A 1-0 win thanks to a Carl Robinson goal rounded off an excellent season.

Photo of the Fulwell End during the 1973 quarter final 2-0 win over Luton, as printed in the semi-final programme v Arsenal at Hillsborough.

Player of the Century 'King' Charlie Hurley and George Forster, doyen of the Sunderland Supporters' Association. Both, in their different ways, embody all that's best about our club and about the game of football.

37 years separate the two photographs from 1968 and 2005.

(Roker Roar magazine)

Living Legends

(Photo A. Brett, courtesy of G. Forster)

(Ken Gambles)

What better way to encourage young fans than for them to meet their heroes?
Claire meets Mickey Gray in 1993/4 and Luke Smith gets to know Julio Arca in 2004/5.

(Lee Smith)

1967/8 1 - 0

1967/8 2 - 1

1969/70 1 - 0

1969/70 1 - 0

1972/3 FA Cup4 3 -1

1980/1 1 - 0

1983/4 2 - 0

1993/4 CocaCola 2 -1

1996/7 3 - 1

1997/8 FA Cup3 5 - 1

1998/9 5 - 2

2000/1 4 - 1

2000/1 4 - 2

2003/4 2 - 0

2004/5 1 - 0

2005/6 2 - 0

Memorable away wins

When we needed a hero

(A.King/G.Biggs)

Marco Gabbiadini

(183 app, 87 g)

Marco's book, Marco in action and a signed picture of Marco playing against some Fat Geordie Bloke

(A.King/G.Biggs)

Sunderland 'til we Die

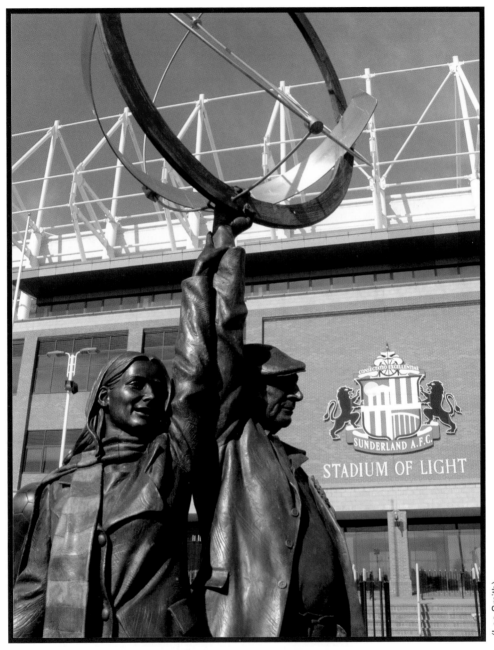

(Lee Smith)

"To be a part of that great history
As those who've gone still are
To take their place with the greatest fans
The world has seen by far."
Alan Craggs

France, skill to die for, had scored in every round so far. All he had to do was beat a badly out of position Bruce Grobbelaar to put us one up. But of course being Sunderland, he couldn't. 0-0 at half-time and I'm sure Malcolm Crosby, the manager's, team talk would have been positive and optimistic. Anyway you know the rest – 2-0 defeat and that old familiar choking lump in the throat.

Homeward bound we passed ex-player Ron Guthrie on the North Circular smiling and waving to fans from his car the size of a time capsule and then the long journey north. The 'sense of humour' of the Notts miners was evident on that banner strung out to taunt us and eventually we reached our local in Darlington at 8.40pm much to the disbelief of the regulars who said we couldn't possibly have been at the game and arrived back in that short length of time.

That was almost the crowning insult, but of course being a Sunderland supporter there had to be a late sting in the tail (or tale) and when I arrived back at home weary and disappointed my thoughtful neighbours had daubed a huge 2-0 in paint on my garage door.

Ha ha ha!

Sat. May 9th 1992   Att. 79,544   Wembley   FA Cup Final
Sunderland 0 v 2 Liverpool
Norman, Owers, Ball, Bennett, Rogan, Rush, Bracewell, Davenport, Armstrong, Byrne, Atkinson. Subs used: Hardyman, Hawke.

Maybe it's because he's a Londoner

Terry Coward, Hartlepool

In today's efficient computerised reliable world of ticket offices it's probably hard to remember just how poor the ticketing system used to be. The Roker ticket office was notorious in the 70s and 80s for its slapdash, annoyingly inept approach so I decided instead to ring Crystal Palace directly to buy tickets for the forthcoming away game on the Saturday at Selhurst Park. Even Roker couldn't match the astonishingly 'professional' charm school treatment I received when I called. The conversation went something like this:

Cockney male voice: "Allo?"

Me: "Do you have any tickets available for Saturday's game against Sunderland?"

Cockney: "Sandland? Fackin' Sandland?"

(Takes phone away from mouth and shouts across room to ticket office colleague)

"Are we playing fackin' Sandland on Sat'day?"

Other Cockney: "Yeah."

Cockney: "How many d'ye want mate?"

You can take the boy out of Sunderland but...

George Booth, Epping

My earliest memories are from the early 1950s. My dad had a couple of season tickets for Roker Park so every home game he and my grandad would be off to the game. I went to reserve games. Each summer would see the ceremony of the collection of the season tickets. This most important visit provided the opportunity to see the large amounts of silverware on display in the trophy cabinets at Roker Park, whose quantity suggested to a young me that we must have won every cup and league that existed. These were on display at the top of the stairs together with that large painting of a hectic goalmouth whose artist enjoyed the splendid name of Thomas Marie Madewaska Hemy. His subject was Sunderland v Aston Villa, Newcastle Road, January 2nd, 1895.

A long time elapsed before my next encounter with this painting on a tour of the SoL in 1999 where it hangs in the main reception area. Casting a more mature eye over the painting raised rather more questions than had been the case with the earlier encounter. Why are there so many players in the goal area? at least 20 on a quick count, why are the lines marking the goal area curved and not straight? why are the Sunderland directors sitting on a bench behind the goal? why is the Sunderland manager shown as one of the linesmen?.....

Other memories from the 1950s include listening to the game against Moscow Dynamo in November 1955. We were listening to commentary on the car radio in the car park at the ground. Now, if my Dad had season tickets, why weren't we in the ground? A question, which now will never be answered. That year my dad won another two season tickets for Roker Park through a competition in the Daily Express. I recall it was his views on the use of floodlights which won this prize. However any hopes of joining him and grandad at home games were quickly dashed when he opted for the cash prize instead 'as he already had enough season tickets'

Family life received a big jolt in 1957 when dad's job changed and we moved to North London. My dad was a ship surveyor and as such was liable to be sent to any of the major ports around the UK. The culture shock of swapping life in Cleadon Village for the bright lights of Enfield and

Southgate in north London was bad enough but, even worse, we were now away fans. Being pitched into the heartlands of Spurs and Arsenal support led to the development of great powers of tact and diplomacy as well as the ability to explain to these good people just where Sunderland was located.

Bleak years followed as dad and I trekked around the south of England as members of a then minority group, Sunderland's travelling support. The 1957/58 season included hearing Luton fans cheer seven times as we lost 7-1 and the final game at Portsmouth which we won but were still relegated. 'Welcome' the banner stretched across the one road into Portsmouth had said, bit of a hollow greeting really. Now I can't remember if it said 'Welcome to Portsmouth' or 'Welcome to Sunderland'. I suppose if they welcomed every visiting side individually they would need at least 20 such banners - oh well. 1958/59 saw us losing by six goals at Fulham and at Leyton Orient with the further joy of six goals against us at Ipswich the following season. We were getting used to this. 1960/61 saw a good cup run which eventually finished with a 6th round reply at a very crowded White Hart Lane where Spurs put 5 goals past us... and then went on to even better things. Inevitably all these visits to other clubs led to us witnessing some of their successes in the league. Thus defeat at Ipswich in April 1961 was the occasion when they won Division 2.

The final game of the following season offered yet another one of those 'if we win and they lose situations then we'll be promoted but...' But indeed. So off we went to Brisbane Road to see the other promotion contenders, Leyton Orient, take on Bury. Now, Bury had a certain Bob Stokoe as player/manager and he was quoted in the press that morning as saying that he wanted to win against Leyton Orient to help Sunderland to gain promotion as they (Sunderland) might spoil Bury's promotion prospects the following season. As a Sunderland fan you know that things never quite go to plan. Sure enough, Sunderland could only draw their game at Swansea and once again we crept out of a ground as the Leyton Orient supporters celebrated getting the promotion place.

Nevertheless the tide had started to turn although the following season saw us just miss promotion (again!) but by 1963/64 we were well on our way. Visiting Brisbane Road again (the O's had come straight down) we relished the sight of the dust rising off the Orient net as Johnny Crossan hammered in a shot to score one of our five goals in a season which ended in our promotion back to the top division.

I move on quickly to 5th May 1973, Cup Final day. What a game, what a day! We went out in high spirits to a Chinese restaurant that evening. 'What are you celebrating?' asked the waiter.

"Sunderland won the Cup," said my mother.

"Your son has won the Cup? That is good," came the reply.

It certainly was.

Belfast Boy   Brian McCullough, Paddock Wood

I have been asked numerous times, "Why do you support Sunderland when you come from Belfast and live in Kent?" Well here is my chance to put the reasons in writing.

The first, and of course only, 'crime' I can remember committing was in the season 1957/1958 at the age of ten. The occasion was the World Cup Qualifying match between Northern Ireland and Italy at Windsor Park, Belfast. My 'crime' was to forge a dental appointment to go home to watch the match on television. The result was a win for Northern Ireland who then famously went on to reach the quarterfinals at the World Cup of 1958 in Sweden.

Playing in that team was Sunderland's Billy Bingham. Hence the awakening of my interest in SAFC, which a few years later grew when N. Ireland internationals Martin Harvey, who replaced captain Danny Blanchflower in the N. Ireland team, and Johnny Crossan both played for Sunderland.

The next stage in the development of my addiction to SAFC came when listening to the radio broadcasts of the FA Cup replays against Manchester United in 1964, but I had to wait until August 1967 before I first had the chance to see the Lads live.

I had taken up a summer holiday job at Butlins Holiday camp at Filey when an early season midweek match at Elland Road gave me the opportunity. (As an aside I met a chap at Butlins called Syd from Consett, who introduced me to N*wc*stl* Brown - I still use the Scottish Breweries bottle opener that he gave me.) Anyway I was able to arrange a day's holiday and set off for Leeds.

I don't expect many people can say that, when they first saw the team that they went on to follow for the rest of their life, they only saw half a game!

Regrettably that was my fate. The reason was that I had to get a bus back to the centre of Leeds, to catch a train to Scarborough, to catch a connection to Filey, to get back to the camp before curfew! Not only that, I had a quick panic when I couldn't find an open exit and 'escaped' Elland Road by climbing through a gap at the top of a turnstile. I am sure I could not do that now - even if there was a big enough gap!

1971 saw me come to live and work in London, which gave me the opportunity to see the Lads whenever they were in town. Unfortunately that did not include going to Wembley in 1973.

My memory of that Cup Final day starts the night before. In a humble bedsit in Mitcham I heard the rain start to fall heavily. I then spent the evening poring over form books for the next day's 2,000 Guineas, looking for a horse who would be suited by the likely soft ground at Newmarket.

The next morning I placed 50p each way on Mon Fils at 100/1 with Mecca Bookmakers and I also had £2 at 11/2 on the lads to beat Leeds in 90 minutes.

What an afternoon I had when Mon Fils won at an SP of 50/1 and Sunderland won 1-0.

My only regret was that sitting alone in my bedsit in front of a second-hand black and white TV there was not a lot of atmosphere! That changed, however, when I met up with a few mates from work for our usual Saturday night in London's West End.

Nowadays I try to get to as many games as possible when the Lads are down south and I usually manage to get to The Stadium of Light at least once a season, keeping in touch with what is going on via the internet, a Programme subscription and, of course, the annual report on my investment of 100 shares in the club.

Like many others I've experienced quite a few ups and downs over the last 40 odd years. Hope springs eternal, however, and here's hoping that 2005/2006 will see us establish ourselves in the Premiership for the long term. Keep the faith!

Devotion or stupidity?   Victoria Clare, Consett

I'm in heaven, all snuggly and warm. My head sunk into my pillow, my teddy by my side and nice and toasty. I have a little smile to myself and sink further into my quilt! Just then I am rudely awakened….by Westlife! It is 7:15 and that is my alarm. For some reason I thought if I changed my alarm from a boring mono-tone beep to a Westlife real-tone it would give me a brighter start to the day-I was wrong as I now realise It gives me no extra incentive to get out of bed! Well they aren't exactly standing there in their suits serenading me so I close my eyes and snooze again!

Next thing I know it is 7:30 and I decide I really should get up. I am going to West Ham for Sunderland's biggest game of the season: win and we will be crowned 'Champions of the Championship' a title, which we crave and want so badly, a title, which we fully deserve. Lose and we will have to face an agonising last game of the season where the title could be snatched from us. I'll ask you the question now-devotion or stupidity travelling ten hours on a bus for ninety minutes of football?….I bet I know what your answer is!

Already the hairs on the back of my neck are standing up, I am so nervous. You see I am a Sunderland fan, but not just an ordinary Sunderland fan. I eat, sleep, drink, dream and live Sunderland AFC, but I can't help it. I have grown up with my dad showing me old videos of past seasons, and as I have had a season ticket since I was six, I unquestioningly devote my Saturdays to football. You know when you walk into someone's house and see pictures of their children or family portraits or a nice landscape…?.Well come into my house and we have the Stadium of Light framed, old Roker Park framed, and memorabilia from when Sunderland beat Newcastle 2-1 for the second year in a row after good old Alan Shearer missed a penalty! Not that I'm complaining, the Stadium of Light has pride of place on my bedroom wall.

My friends don't seem to understand....while they're out shopping, I'm at the Stadium of Light or some football ground round the country, and while Brad and Jude are the main feature on their bedroom walls, they take a back seat in my room to make way for my Sunderland heroes! They think I waste my time....I am a girl....who likes football....but it's for boys....so I must only go to watch their legs surely?!? If I'm truly honest, Id be lying if I said part of that wasn't true. Sometimes when it's a boring game and not much is happening I do have a little look at the players' legs, just like the lads will have a look at the girls sitting around them! But most people find it hard to understand my knowledge and love of the game-it's my passion. I can put the boys to shame in any argument but they don't listen to me....because I'm a girl-what do I know? I usually respond with the challenge, "Come back to me and have a go at me when you travel all over the country to watch your team". That usually shuts them up.

Anyway I must stop my mind wandering as it is now 7:45 and I have just looked in the mirror and my hair resembles a lion's mane .It needs serious straightening. While I sort that out my mam brings me a bacon sandwich and a cup of tea, after which I proceed with my make-up routine: moisturiser, foundation, powder, blusher, eye shadow, mascara and lip-gloss. My dad looks on in amazement. "You're only going to a football game," he says.

But I like to look nice-never know who you'll meet....I've always wanted to be a footballer's wife! I ping my home shirt off its hanger, put on my favourite pair of jeans, and then hunt out my gorgeous pink baseball boots to complete my match day outfit.

Before I know it its 9:30 and my lift has arrived. I slouch out of the door still half asleep, say bye to my mam and shuffle to the car. I have a fifteen minute drive to Stanley picking up two more of my dad's friends along the way and then at ten o'clock we board the bus. I sit by the window because I love to watch the scenery and wave at other Sunderland fans making their way to the game. I occasionally give the odd sarcastic wave to the Newcastle fans as well!

Just as I get myself comfortable it dawns on me I am going to be stuck on this bus for five hours! Devotion or stupidity? At this minute for me it's still devotion! My friend Peter sits next to me to keep me company. However we always end up driving each other crazy.

For the next two hours I have to listen to nine men discussing and analysing last week's game and how the referee is a disgrace to the footballing industry. On the way down I start to think-would I like to give up going to the football for shopping all day? Part of me wishes that I could spend more time with my friends over the weekend but then I get a flashback of how stressed I became that Saturday when there was no football and I decided to go the Metro Centre-BIG mistake! I didn't spend any money that day but I did spend a lot of time being dodged out of the way by raving mad women with daddy's money to spend and then when I did find a lovely pair of jeans I stormed out of the shop in a huff....that label said size 12....they very clearly weren't!

Yet again I stop my daydreaming and decide to kill some time by blasting out some music on my Walkman. It works as the next thing I know we are at a small café for a stop-off and some food. I'm not impressed. I wander straight in and straight back out. The thought of any food just turns my stomach, so instead I join everyone outside in the sunshine. Then I resign myself to another two hours back on the bus before we get to the pub. The journey is bearable although I am slightly tired. The only saving grace is that this is a night kick-off....if it had been a three o'clock kick-off I don't think I would have been able to cope with getting up at four in the morning.

The tension is growing on the bus, so many emotions: nerves, tension and excitement. As the last hour of the journey approaches we stop at a service station where I sit outside soaking up the sunshine and atmosphere whilst my dad buys me a Solero .As I look around, I see the M25 service station has been over run with Sunderland fans. I think it's fair to say most of them are fairly tipsy....and who can blame them! I glance around and look at so many different people all here for one reason. You can see the nerves on people's faces, although it's not as bad as last week. You see we have already secured promotion we just want to seal it in style.

Once again we board the bus to continue the final part of our journey. As we arrive in London I stare out of the window where I can see Upton Park's roof peering above the buildings. As I get off the bus the ground is gradually growing....along with my nerves. The atmosphere in the pub is electric with hundreds of Sunderland fans singing, dancing, drinking and just generally having a good time. Some are dressed as Elvis, some are dressed as doctors and nurses, some are dressed as pirates but the majority of them are wearing their red and white shirts and wearing them with pride again. Sitting around the table I suddenly realise the disadvantage of being the only girl in a group of ten. The programme man comes round and asks if anyone would like a match day programme, and five people buy one including me. After a quick flick through I put it in my bag, a move that is shortly followed by:

"Is there room for mine?"

"Would you keep mine please Vicky?"

"Erm....yeah actually mine too?"

"Well you might as well keep mine then!"

I now have five programmes in my bag. I hope I don't get searched….I might look a bit suspicious.

We start our wander along to the ground shortly after, the Sunderland and West Ham fans mixing together and having a bit of friendly banter. However you can see what they really mean when they say 'good luck mate'- 'I hope we beat you good and proper'. There is a lot at stake in this game, we have to win to secure the Championship, but West Ham have to win to ensure their place in the play-offs. It is going to be no walkover for either team.

Now I make my way to the turnstiles the deafening sounds of 'Sunderland's going up' ringing in my ears. My bag does get searched but they don't notice my library of programmes although I do get my bottle top taken off me. I hand in my ticket slip and clunk my way through the turnstiles. Now I have to get rid of my half drunk bottle of blackcurrant and I don't particularly want it all so Peter and I find a novel way of getting rid of it-by having a blackcurrant fight.

Once that is sorted I have to fight my way through a sea of people, furiously dodging flying beer that is being spilt. I have my Consett flag wrapped around my shoulders and am holding tightly onto my dad's hand so I don't get lost as I climb up the stairs of block Y. The sight of thirty three thousand people in the ground make the hairs on the back of my neck stand up. You can almost see the nerves bouncing off the walls as I find my seat and stand for a while gazing round the stands. I take a deep breath. This is it- now! Part of me wants to run out of the ground but I know I can't and really don't want to.

The teams run out in front of their faithful fans. The sound is so deafening, I can't even hear the West Ham fans. I'm now so involved in saluting my Sunderland heroes that for a split second I forget about the game. West Ham play their club song while the Sunderland fans try to block it out by singing their own songs and now the whole ground is so unbelievably loud I don't even realise the game has kicked off!

Not much happens in the first half. We play satisfactorily but every time the ball goes into either half I can't bear to watch, I think I see more of Peter's shoulder than the game in the first half. I know it sounds silly but in my head if I can't see it, it's not happening. Still I'm sure everyone has moments like that! The clock shows forty-three minutes so I think we're safe….until half time at least.

How very wrong I am! Marlon Harewood shoots, the ball hits the post and crosses the line, West Ham one Sunderland nil. I stand still, frozen to the spot. I can't write down what is going through my head. I have my head in my hands. I think I am still standing in the same place when the half time whistle blows. I hadn't thought about us losing .All I had thought about was how fantastic it will be when we win. We can't lose. We just can't!!

I find it hard to put into words how disappointed I am. The only way I can describe it is to say it's like some one was about to give you a big trophy filled with gold and you are so close to it you can touch it, but someone makes you take one step back. People find it hard to understand how emotionally involved I get-but it's true. It's got to be affecting my health! Even though I feel so disappointed, I refuse to give up hope. I know we can still do it. I have every faith in the team and know they will do everything they can to ensure they do not let the fans down. A loud cheer greets the players as they come back onto the pitch.

Everyone is as optimistic as I am and we continue singing. It doesn't take long for Sunderland to equalise though it's the sloppiest goal I've ever seen in my life, possibly an own goal: however do we care?! Two thousand five hundred Sunderland fans now start the chant, "Championes,

Championes, ole, ole, ole.' However I refuse to join in. I don't tempt fate, as we technically aren't champions yet.

The tension is really growing. We need another goal, and there are thirty minutes left. The time ticks away. As every minute passes my nerves grow. When it gets to eighty - seven minutes, I think, 'Come on please, please, please just score.' Just then Ben Alnwick takes a goal kick. It goes down the field and Chris Brown heads it down for Stephen Elliot who keeps running. We all stand.

"He's going to score here....I know it," says my dad. "He's going to do it." We all freeze for what seems like an eternity. Stephen Elliot shoots. We've scored. Everything's going right....the Sunderland fans are sent into a state of delirium again and we all start jumping about.

Just then I feel a blow to my face and I fall back onto my chair. My nose has been hit. My eyes start furiously filling up with water as I drag myself up to celebrate the goal. I am in so much pain. I feel something trickle down my nose. "Oh no my nose is running and I don't have a tissue." I try to stop it with my hand and that's when I realise....it's blood, I'm having a nosebleed and it won't stop. It's like a tap. My dad, Peter and his dad realising I'm not celebrating all turn round to hug me but freeze on the spot when they see my bloodied face. My dad hands me a hanky as the Sunderland fans are still going mental!

Things get even worse as the totally gorgeous lad from three rows in front of me has somehow found his way to the row in front of mine. He turns round to give me a 'yes we've done it kiss' but the look of excitement and happiness soon turns to horror and he just manages to mutter the words, "Eeeh are you all right pet?" I say yes but my blood stained lips and nose suggest otherwise and he turns back round quickly.

Everyone around me is noticing my nosebleed and they all start asking me if I'm ok. I feel bad as they should be celebrating the goal, not fussing over me! I can't believe my luck-the most important goal of the season and I can't celebrate it....well I am going to. I start jumping up and down and singing but have to stop as it is not helping matters!

The next three minutes are a blur. As I'm still trying to stop my nose bleeding, I'm not aware of anything going on around me ….. until the referee puts up four minutes stoppage time FOUR MINUTES?! I knew he was a West Ham fan! I can honestly say I have never known a longer four minutes in my life it seemed like four hours! Finally the sound I have been waiting to hear all day is heard-the final whistle! I now join in the celebrations, regardless of the pain I am in. This is what I have been waiting for all season, and nothing is going to stop me. I stand on my chair with my dad and happily join in the Champions' Chant as yet again the Sunderland fans are sent into delirium.

I ask myself the question devotion or stupidity again? I have to admit when I was hit the answer was definitely stupidity but as soon as I see my Sunderland team applauding me it turns to devotion again. I have tears in my eyes and it's not because of my nose: it's pride! The team stays out in front of the fans for about twenty minutes before returning to party in their dressing room.

Two thousand five hundred Sunderland fans stay in the ground for at least half an hour....singing to no one in particular and hugging, kissing and celebrating with people that they've never met before in their life! When we finally leave the ground and board the buses I am slightly tired but nothing is going to wipe that big cheesy grin off my face. I sleep most of the way back, and even though everyone is ecstatic at first it soon becomes quiet as it is three o'clock and we are still on the road. The journey seems to drag on and on and on but I eventually get back home at four thirty in the morning.

When I get into bed at five o'clock. I reflect on my day. This trip has been one of my best. I had already planned that I was going to wear my Sunderland strip all week. It represents pride again and I find great amusement in the fact that Newcastle are struggling at the bottom of the Premiership.

I lie in my bed staring at my Sunderland posters, fourteen players are on my door, my champions: I have just travelled ten hours on a bus to watch them; I will be getting up in five hours time to watch their television appearance; I had my nose bust watching them; and I spend my weekends devoting myself to the club.

I move to my wall where I have my collection of match tickets twenty-four away tickets are on display from the past two seasons. I have been to twenty-five different grounds around the country. I then look at my collection of photographs. There are fifty-six on display, twenty-nine of them show me either with a Sunderland player or wearing Sunderland clothing. Would I change or do I regret any of this? No it's my life, my passion. I'd be lost without it. Now decide - devotion or stupidity?

Fri. April 29th 2003   Att. 33,842   Upton Park   Championship
West Ham United 1 v 2 Sunderland
(Arca, Elliott)
Alnwick, Wright, Breen, Caldwell, McCartney, Lawrence, Robinson, Whitehead, Arca, Stewart, Brown. Subs used: Elliott, Deane, Collins.

Quiz 4

Monty's Name The Ground posers

The current division (2005/6) is in brackets following the clue.

(Answers on p 128)

1   Princess's meadow? (Premiership)

2   Stadium to rule the waves? (Championship)

3   Tree spring? (Championship 1)

4   Arena for pedestrians? (Champ 1)

5   Half a dozen grassy areas? (Champ 2)

6   Turnips, swedes and potatoes at big house. (Champ 1)

7   Ascot? (Champ 2)

8   Place of a deadly sin. (Champ)

9   Capital way? (Champ 2)

10   Zit country? (Champ 2)

11   Fruit you can't reach. (Prem)

12   Thoroughfare for watching an Ashes Test? (Champ 2)

13   Used to leave his car there? (Prem)

14   Sounds like the girl was aware? (Champ)

15   Lichen went higher? (Champ 2)

Hammered

Peter Barker, Billingham

Living in London in the late sixties an away match in the capital was always something to really look forward to. We were usually well beaten at all the London grounds (so what's changed?) but at least it gave you a chance to see the Lads and get your 'football fix' for relatively little money. Football was still cheap in those days and very much a working class sport still.

We were playing West Ham at Upton Park – every chance of getting something from the game – Bobby Moore, Geoff Hurst, Martin Peters, World Cup Winners all, but so what? they weren't all that good surely?

The day started badly. I left New Cross in South London and changed tubes at Whitechapel. I'd only booked as far as Whitechapel but as a tube for Upton Park was waiting I jumped on intending to pay at the other end (honest!) Anyway despite this genuine mistake I was caught without a ticket and summoned to appear at London Transport Police at Kings Cross at a later date. Never mind, at least there was the game to look forward to…

West Ham 8 v 0 Sunderland

(Geoff Hurst 6)

Standing on the tube station afterwards totally fed up and thinking things couldn't get much more depressing, two East End skinheads (remember them?) gave me a slap in the mouth and nicked my Sunderland scarf. All the rage in those days.

So what a day – got nicked, got stuffed and got mugged all in dedication to the cause of SAFC. Why do we do it?

Not a total disaster, for the Old Bill swallowed the genuine mistake story and I was a free man, ready for the next defeat in the Smoke.

Sat. Oct 19th 1968   Att. 24,903   Upton Park   Division 1

West Ham United 8 v 0 Sunderland

Montgomery, Irwin, Palmer, Hurley, Harvey, Porterfield, Herd, Harris, Brand, Suggett, Mulhall.

One Wedding and a Final

Claire Gambles, Secretary North Yorkshire Branch, SAFCSA

My Dad's loves in life are: my mum (of course), beer, cricket, food and football (not necessarily in that order...sorry mum!) and his dislikes are; Newcastle United, people who walk slowly, Blind Date and Musicals. Although he obviously dislikes Newcastle far more than any of the above, for the purpose of my story I will focus on the last point. My Dad can't understand why in musicals, mundane conversation has to be sung and he cannot suspend his disbelief far enough to accept that the characters suddenly know all the words and dance routines when they have only just met! So, when it came to the 3rd Round of the FA Cup in 1992 he must have been fairly certain of an early exit for Sunderland, when he confidently announced he would take me, my mum and my sister to see a musical in London if they made it to the final! Lo and behold, quicker than that fabulous Gordon Armstrong header, he found himself sitting in a theatre in the West End in May enduring Andrew Lloyd Webber's 'Starlight Express'!

Keeping the faith is always important, but for most teams, cup runs do not happen often and free Saturdays on cup days are usually very common for Sunderland Supporters. Because of this I was not unduly worried when my boyfriend's sister announced her wedding was to be on 2004 Cup Final day at three o'clock and I was only slightly concerned when she confirmed the hen night would be in Belgium on the Semi Final weekend!

So, along with everyone else when the FA Cup came round in 2004 I enjoyed the win against Hartlepool and revelled in the surprise win at Ipswich. But as Sunderland progressed further into the competition I began to grow more and more anxious. I have had a season ticket for over ten years and after witnessing the abysmal seventeen successive defeats I desperately wanted to witness the good times if we were to embark on a cup run. When we drew Birmingham I was sure the run would end so I would be able to relax and look forward to the wedding, but by the time we had earned a replay I was seriously struggling to get behind the Lads. Instead of going barmy when we won I found myself collapsing and shouting, 'I bloody knew it!' as I pictured my ecstatic Dad at the Millennium Stadium without me. Selfishly I could hardly bear for Sunderland to reach the Cup Final if I was not going to be there. After beating Sheffield United in the quarter final there was a good chance that this really was going to happen and by now I knew there was nothing I could do about it.

Well, as I suppose I should have expected, Semi Final day arrived and I found myself in Brussels not Old Trafford, Manchester, with 3 girls....2 of whom loathed football! I decided to target the girl who liked football early on in the weekend and selfishly arranged that we would find a pub with SKY TV and watch the match whilst the bride to be and bridesmaid hit the shops and sampled the Belgian chocolate. I'm sure it would have been easier for everyone involved if I'd avoided the football altogether but for some insane reason I just had to watch it and learn our fate.

After a delicious meal and a rather heavy night out, the big morning eventually arrived and all I wanted was to be sitting in front of the big screen with a Belgian beer ready to cheer the lads on and accept the result. However 'the hens' seemed to be taking ages to get ready and girl I had managed to poach had been in the toilet for a suspiciously long time. I tried to rally everyone around without making them wish I hadn't been invited and eventually we made it to the tube station. Once we were safely on board I began to relax knowing I was one step closer, until my new footballing partner suddenly announced that last night's delicious meal had not agreed with her and she needed to get off the tube immediately. No, no no! I had only just got everyone on the tube and now we were all tumbling off at some random station in the middle of Belgium's capital mere minutes before kick off!

Looking like the Scooby Doo gang on a mission I joined in the stampede and ran as fast as I could, knowing that not finding a toilet would only slow us down further! Unfortunately the only toilet in our deserted station was locked and we wasted even more valuable minutes trying to obtain a key from someone who did not understand the phrase 'in a hurry' or in fact any English whatsoever. At this moment my sympathies should have been with the poor suffering soul who was about to enter this dark and dingy place, but all I could do was look at my watch as I begrudgingly realised my chance of witnessing kick off was slipping away minute by minute.

Eventually after a loud and long summit meeting it was decided that the bridesmaid would stretcher the 'injured hen' off to the apartment leaving me with the not so satisfactory substitute of a bride who hated football. Twenty minutes after kick off, we finally made it to an Irish pub where I found we were already 1-0 down. I felt gutted that we were losing, yet strangely pleased that it had kicked off and I had no control over the result. I hated admitting it but I was so nervous that I still could potentially miss the final.

As you all know I needn't have worried. When the final whistle went I was really disappointed for the players and supporters but relieved I would not be missing potentially one of the biggest days in my footballing history. Instead I attended the biggest day in my boyfriend's sister's life and as she walked down the aisle to greet her future husband, I smiled somewhat thankfully as I pictured my dad glum, but safely at home in front of the television, and a Millennium stadium free of red and white striped shirts!

Sun. April 4th 2004   Att. 56,112   Old Trafford   FA Cup Semi
Millwall 1 v 0 Sunderland
Poom, Wright, Breen, Babb, McCartney, Oster, McAleer, Thirlwell, Arca, Kyle, Smith. Subs used: Piper, Stewart, Thornton.

Answers to Monty's Quizzes

Quiz 1   True or False

1) T   2) F   3) F   4) T   5) F   6) T   7) F   8) T   9) F   10) F   11) F   12) T

13) T   14) F   15) T   16) F   17) T   18) F   19) T   20) F

Quiz 2   Find the Pairs

Phillips – Elvis   (supporter dressed as Elvis paid homage after hat-trick at Bradford)

Reid – yard dog scrapper   (described as such by Bill Shankly)

McMenemy – white handkerchief   (waved after surviving relegation 1986)

Kay – tractor   (Howard Wilkinson said of Kay's tackle on Haddock – it was like he'd been run over by a tractor)

Arca – jellyfish   (stung by one in training session at Seaburn)

McAteer – autobiography   (taunted Roy Keane during game saying, "Put it in your book!")

Shepherd – dog   (described Newcastle women as 'dogs')

Martin Smith – Pele's son   (Fans' nickname 'son of Pele')

Bob Stokoe - trilby

Len Shackleton – a blank page   (in his autobiography to show a Chairman's knowledge about football)

Craig Russell – the Jarrow Arrow

Jody Craddock – a painting   (he is an accomplished artist)

Baxter – The Roker Hotel   (a favourite drinking spot)

Willie Watson – cricket bat   (played test cricket as well as football for England)

Quiz 3   Cryptic Player

1) Gary <u>Owers</u>   2) Ian <u>Sampson</u>   3) Brian <u>Usher</u>   4) Brett <u>Angell</u>   5) Alf <u>Common</u>   6) Harry <u>Hood</u>   7) Peter <u>Daniel</u>   8) Paul <u>Lemon</u>   9) Kevin <u>Ball</u> 10) Colin <u>Todd</u>   11) Keith <u>Coleman</u>   12) Bob <u>Bolder</u>

Quiz 4   Name the Ground posers

1) Anfield (Anne-field) 2) Brittania   3) Oakwell 4) Walkers 5) Sixfields 6) Roots Hall 7) Racecourse Ground   8) Pride Park 9) London Road   10) Spotland   11) Highbury (High-berry)   12) Brisbane Road   13) Ewood Park (He would park)   14) Molineux (Molly knew)   15) Moss Rose

That's Hall folks!

Fred Hall – Post-war stalwart, skipper and centre half. A tremendous servant to the club, he played 224 times, scoring his only goal on Christmas Day 1953 in the 1-1 draw with Huddersfield Town.

(Signed photo donated by Campbell family, Catchgate)

The Spirit of Wearside

Alan Craggs, Aberdeen

I was there at the end in '97, when tears blurred my sight.
We were leaving good old Roker for the Stadium of Light.
I never knew how I'd miss the place, how it would be so sore.
Like things in life that are never missed, until they're there no more.

I went back to Roker Park, loads of times, to see the Park pulled down.
Took pictures while remembering the place that was the crown
Of Sunderland Association Football Club, for so long the place of dreams
Of those of All the Talents and Bank of England teams.
Of Championships and heroes, of cup ties and of Kings,
Of massive crowds and it all meant to be proud of all those things.
But it was gone my Roker, it was gone when I was there,
As I looked upon the houses that are built around the square.

I looked, and as I turned to go an old man blocked my way.
I apologised, but he just said in friendly tones, "Ha'way,
Nee problem, young 'un, just a bump, a'ye down te see the grund?
Whey, there's stories A c'n tell ye, but ye knaa that now ye've fund
The greatest place a bodies seen in the hist'ry o' the game.
W've had ou' ups and downs like, but we loved it just the same."
This man looked grey, and from a time that was so long ago.
With his flat cap, boots and overcoat, he shone an ancient glow.

"A've seen thousands 'ere son, massive crowds, ower seventy five one time.
That was then, but, dear me, a mountain we would climb
For all the lads that gave tha' guts in the shirts of red and white.
W'd put arl the other football teams inter fits of sheer fright.
Look at all the folk wees done tha' bit in Roker's time.

From back in the eighteen seventies, auld Sun'land's been se grand,
It's nee wonder that around the world ye'll get a Sun'land hand
Te talk of goals and special teams and away games wi' tha' mates,
Or seein' the last ten minutes free when the've opened all the gates."

I couldn't believe I was speaking with a man with memories that
Could bring back all the details of where Roker's glories sat.
I told him even I'd been there before the Clockstand seats went in
Or the Fulwell roof built overhead to keep us from the rain.

A chuckle then and the old man said, "Aye, before the big World Cup,
But A c'n tell ye 'bout the years we were always lookin' up.
Think about all Sun'lands greatest names that played right here.
There's memories a' plenty, but more important and more dear
Was the crowd at Roker, and that noise, no other could surpass.
Whey, th'd turn out in tha' thousands just for striped shirts on the grass.
Th've seen the best, th've beat the best, the noise would bust a door.
Th've been the best, need to be the best, they were Wearside's Roker Roar.
Aye, the sound was deaf'nin, a legend even now.
No club has ever beaten that famous Sunderland row."
I smiled now at the man, "Aye, no doubt it was the best!"
He smiled back, saying simply, "But remember all the rest
That have gone before, tha'ashes spread where possible on the green
Of the best-supported football club the world has ever seen.
Th're all still there behind the team through times both good and bad,
And you c'n bet tha' spirit's always right there with the lads."

I asked him to tell me of a time when glory filled the ground,
"It's comin' son and A'll tell ye now, it'll be better this time 'round.
But all ye lads and lasses don't forget what's all gone by,
'Cos there's a massive Sun'land back up, in the Stadium in the sky.

Listen to the bedlam we were all part of in the past.

A noise, louder than the others, that will forever last

As a legend in the stories of football stadiums grand;

That ear splittin' roar of the name of Sunderland.

We'll always be there with ye, the spirits cry the name

Of Sunderland forever, of the best fans in the game.

Listen to our nature, of the world that needs to scream.

The sound or roarin' in the sky motivates our team.

Now remember what A've told ye, niver doubt the sounds ye hear.

Borne on wind and darkness, all but Sun'land fans will fear."

He looked beyond me, smiling then, recognition on his face.

"A ye gannin' ower, bonny lads, w'll ha' te run te get ou' place."

I quickly turned to who'd replied in whispered tones, "Why aye."

But no-one stood there, not one soul as the darkness stole the sky.

And behind the darkness came a wind, with voices in its throat.

A swelling, thundering, all surrounding, overwhelming note.

It came on the wind that strengthened as it rustled at the trees

Moving everything before it, a crescendo through the leaves.

As I stood transfixed, I heard them come, whole families, Sons and Dads.

A million ghostly voices screamed as one

"Ha'way the Lads."

My hair and clothes were pulled and whipped as I fought to keep my feet,

Brushed by countless misty bodies as they bustled down the street.

Young and old, large and small, their faces all one way,

Set with expectation for how the Lads would play that day.

In the deafening storm, I turned again, but the man was there no more.

He'd returned to take his place within that heavenly Roker Roar.

With all the supporters past and gone, the volume building fast,
Looking on and bellowing with the players of the past.
All touched by the magic born in Sunderland's little plot.
All now fiercely loyal, whether from the Wear or not.
The roar rolled on before me, it was a fearsome sound
But it settled back to quiet as it passed beyond the ground.

So, remember, it's not a legend, it's real like me and you.
We're all Sunderland, 'till we die, but it goes beyond that too.
Lest we forget, we must ensure our babies know the stories;
Great players past and characters, the heartbreak and the glories.
Whilst they, no doubt, will have success abundant in their days,
And the Stadium of Light will fill with sound and winning ways,
Once in a while tell them to heed when a storm comes in the night
And to face the wind of voices, to feel the awesome might.
To be part of that great history, as those who have gone still are.
To take their place with the greatest fans the world has seen by far.
To sing their hearts out for the Lads with the spirits in the dark.
To keep the Wearside memories of glorious Roker Park.

We are Sunderland

Together to the future

As publishers of quality books, we have three main aims. Firstly, PDG Books is committed to promoting writing in any genre or style which is distinctive, thought-provoking and readable. Work which interests us is situated between the extremes of "literary" and "populist" so if your preference, as a reader or as a writer, is for books which are a pleasure to read but have hidden depths then our titles will be of interest to you. Secondly, PDG Books is committed to a wide range of voices, visions and points of view. We value but don't insist on writing being "cool" or "cutting edge" and we don't reject good work just because the values it promotes have been around for a long time. This means that for many people PDG Books represents a rare opportunity to write and to read the kinds of books you like best. Thirdly, PDG Books is committed to a co-operative and proactive approach to both producing and selling books. If you are a writer with an idea that we wish to take forward we will, if needed, work with you to develop your writing to a publishable quality. If you are a reader we will take great interest in your tastes and opinions and will listen to and act upon any criticisms or recommendations you send to us.